*I would like to dedicate this book to my
beautiful, supportive and loving wife,
Kristine who continues to make my
life so very special, every day.*

*To my daughters Mazana and Isabella,
for the endless joy that you bring into our lives.*

*And to my sister in-law, Jill Price who has
pushed me to take the time to write this book.
I appreciate your invaluable daily efforts,
your unwavering commitment and
sincere ongoing support.*

Investment Tools to grow you and your business...

Creating Loyal Profitable Customers Manual

If you want to take your business to the next level of success, this program is a must. A two-hour video, 2 x 60 min audio-tape with a comprehensive Customer Loyalty manual. You will discover leading-edge business building strategies, whether you are a Sales Person, Manager, Executive, Home-Based Business Owner, Customer Service Person, Franchisee or Entrepreneur.
AUS $295.00 plus GST

Creating Loyal Profitable Customers Video

'How to double your income without double the effort.'
This two hour live presentation promotes profitable business growth techniques and simple specific strategies that will make all the difference in bringing your customers back time and time again. With Workbook.
AUS$100 plus GST

Creating Loyal Profitable Customers Audio

'How to double your income without double the effort.'
This two pack audio program shows you the simple step by step formula for gaining an endless supply of referrals, how to develop and implement a business growth plan using the multiplying factor to double your income plus many more time proven strategies to create loyal profitable customers.
AUS$79.00 plus GST.

Goal Setting Video

This one-hour video will inspire you to make it happen. In a nutshell, you get the easy-to-implement steps of goal setting. You will also learn a goal setting model that will clarify your long and short vision, how to have self-mastery in every area of your personal and professional life.
With Workbook. AUS $100.00 plus GST.

Goal Setting Audio

These two 60 min tapes are packed with hints, tips and strategies that make your dreams that much more real and attainable. You will discover how to develop unwavering personal focus in everything you do, the 10 ways to enhance personal esteem and self-confidence, plus many more strategies to overcome any obstacle that stops you achieving your full potential.
AUS $40.00 plus GST.

To grab a copy of your favourite investment tool ring 61 7 3848 5646 or visit www.keithabraham.com.au and buy on our secure server.

Creating Loyal Profitable Customers

47 ways to turn your customers into passionate purchasers

KEITH ABRAHAM
CERTIFIED SPEAKING PROFESSIONAL

AUSTRALIAN BEST SELLER

"If you don't invest time and money in yourself, you are a poor judge of a good investment"

Second reprint 2000

Third reprint 2001

Published in Brisbane, Australia by People Pursuing A Passion Pty Ltd.

Distributed by Gary Allen Pty Ltd

ISBN: 0-646-37583-0

CONTENTS

Creating Loyal Profitable Customers

47 ways to turn your customers into passionate purchasers

T E S T I M O N I A L S

What our Clients say...

"Keith not only delivers a powerful and energetic presentation, but he also provides credible follow-up and support mechanisms so that the team obtains consistent reinforcement of his message. Keith also challenged us to strive for the next level. He introduced a whole new way of approaching the development of the business by encouraging us to think about what we could achieve if there were no barriers to success."
Ian Andrew, General Manager - Personalised Plates Queensland

"With customers the life-blood of business today it makes good business sense to maintain your client base. Loyalty is the only way to do this! Keith, you have set the benchmark for customer loyalty with your own professional style and the effective strategies that you introduce into your clients organisations."
Robyn Henderson CSP, Global Networking Specialist, International keynote speaker, business educator and author

"Your attendance and involvement at our conference was the best investment we have ever made in the last 8 conferences. Your involvement assisted greatly in our delegates going back to their offices and making change, and have shown substantial growth."
Andrew Challinor, State Manager - UTAG

"Your presentation was sharp, witty and importantly relative to critical aspects of our business. Your PowerPoint presentation connected strongly with your personal approach to our team members."
Rob Morgan, Director - SPORTSCO

Need a Speaker for your next Conference?

Keynote and Workshops Topics

Creating Loyal Customers
Designing Your Life
Memorable Marketing
Strategic Selling

To book Keith for a conference or workshop, speak to us on 61 7 3848 5646 or visit www.keithabraham.com.au.

INTRODUCTION

Getting the most out of this book to maximise your return on investment

"If you don't invest time, energy and money in yourself - you are a poor judge of a good investment."

Congratulations on investing time, energy and money in yourself and on your business. This book is about giving you the edge over your competitors so that you can develop a unique point-of-difference in your marketplace that will set you apart. As a result people will want to do business with you and in turn, bring their friends with them. Throughout this book we will explore a number of tools, techniques, ideas, information and strategies on how you can dominate your marketplace by giving your customers more reasons to return to your business.

You see, I don't think we give our customers enough reasons to return to our businesses. Good service just won't cut it any more. It is about creating a customer loyalty system that consistently communicates with our customers so that we are at the top of their minds. I also think that our customers, as well as you and I, experience so much poor customer service in the marketplace that it is really easy to create a point-of-difference that gets people to return to our businesses and become loyal advocates of our products and services.

We are living on the edge of the information super highway. It's time we got out of the emergency breakdown lane and into the fast lane of success. I know you would have realised that, to compete in today's marketplace you need to be better, faster and have a point-of-difference that is unique, interesting and inviting. Now more than ever we need to move from being a Product Provider to becoming a Service Partner.A Product Provider just sells a product with little or no service.A Service Provider sells a product and gives some service. But the service is just acceptable, not exceptional. It does not create a memorable experience for the customer. A Service Partner, on the other hand, is someone who knows who their customers are, what they do and how they like to be served. They give their customers a positive experience that they can rave about to their friends which keeps them coming back because the Service Partner gives them a reason to return.

Product Provider ---> Service Provider ---> Service Partner

Your success in business in this ever-shrinking global marketplace we live and work in will depend on your ability and willingness to change with the times.This book will give you the tools to fine-tune your business, so that you can travel at the speed of sound on today's business super highway.

Today our customers are more astute, more demanding and have more choices than ever before.That's why you need to work smarter and spend time on the things that count.You need to focus all your energies on the activities that build your business by gaining greater customer loyalty.

In the following pages you will find market tested hints and tips you can implement today, with little or no effort. You will find strategies that will revolutionise your business forever.As well as discovering proven, easy to implement business formulas.You will also review tools and techniques to make your business even more profitable.These strategies are about taking your business, yourself and your people to the next level in your marketplace.

This book has ten chapters, which are outlined in a specifically designed model for you to follow (see below). On the following page I have given you an insight into what you can expect from each chapter.

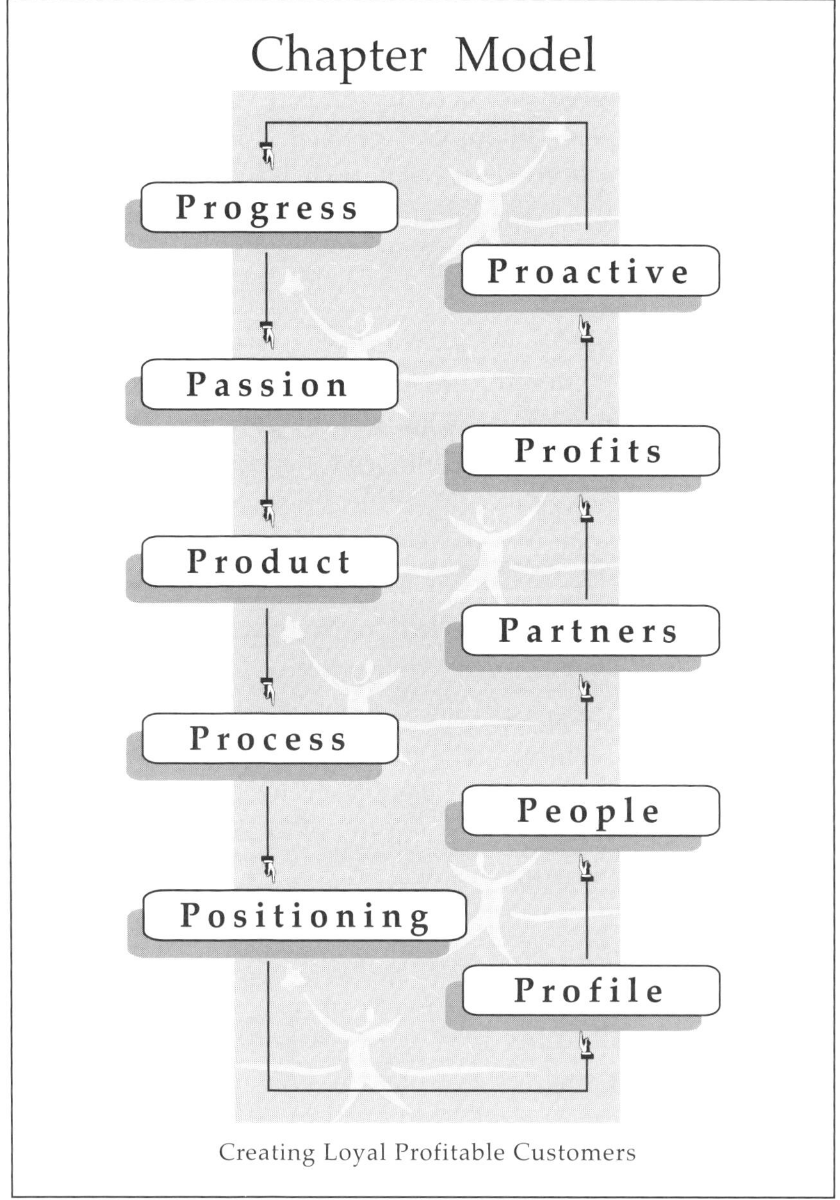

Chapter 1. *Progress - Change before you need to change*
Change is sometimes the hardest thing to do. We will talk about where you are at now and what you need to change to capitalise on the future. I will share with you how to make that transition in your business.

Chapter 2. *Passion - Finding a passion worth pursuing*
Today we need to be driven by a passion to be significant in our marketplace. This chapter gives you a simple formula to identify where you want to be and how to get there in the shortest possible time.

Chapter 3. *Product - What business are you really in?*
Sometimes the product you are selling is not the product people want to buy. We will define the real business your customers want you to be in now, the business of creating a service selling experience that they will rave about.

Chapter 4. *Process - Creating a Service Selling System with personality*
Systems drive businesses, but people drive the systems. This chapter looks at the processes that ensure your customers receive a great service experience. We will explore every step and strategy to make the processes work in your business.

Chapter 5. *Positioning - Creating a unique point of difference that sets you apart*
We all know how to work hard. Now it's time to work smarter by knowing what type of customers you want and how to maximise your business profitability, by taking advantage of the opportunities that exist within your current business.

Chapter 6. *Profile - Creating a customer loyalty system that works in your business*
I will share with you 47 tried and proven ways to create customer loyalty in your business. This chapter is information-rich and strategy-specific when it comes to building and maintaining customer loyalty in your marketplace.

Chapter 7. *People - Are your people focused on what counts?*
This chapter looks at how to get the right people doing the right job with the right results. It gives you a number of easy to-implement tools to use to get your people committed to giving great customer service.

Chapter 8. *Partners - Building strategic alliances that add value to your customers*
Your business can be a lonely place sometimes. We will identify whom to target as your strategic partners so that everyone benefits - you, your customers and your strategic partners.

Chapter 9. *Profits - At the end of the day are you making a profit?*
Profitability is king. We will review a simple model which will show you how you can almost double your income without doubling the effort and have your customers happy to pay.

Chapter 10. *Proactive - It's not what you say, it's what you do that counts*
In today's business world you are either: reactive, adaptive or proactive. We will look at ways you can take these loyalty gaining strategies and become a proactive player in your marketplace.

How to get the most out this book

What amazes me is that so few people read books. I heard an interesting statistic that only 30% of books purchased are ever read and, of that 30%, only 40% of people ever get past chapter 3.

I know you want to maximise your potential and that of your business. My goal is to make this book a practical insight with easy-to-implement strategies, as well as to provide you with an inspirational experience along the way. I have written this book with a number of exercises for you to complete as you progress through it.

That's why 'Creating Loyal Profitable Customers' is about thinking, creating, planning and achieving your business goals. The questions I will ask you are designed to make you think about your business, your role and your purpose for being in business. They have been specifically designed to make you think about where your business is going.

12-Month Electronic Loyalty Learning Program

I have also set up a specific electronic coaching program to help you implement your favourite loyalty gaining ideas. All you need to do is go to my website at http://www.keithabraham.net.au and log on to the weekly loyalty ideas. By the way, you will need a password to receive this weekly idea for the next 52 weeks. That password is: Loyal Customers.

The Bottom Line - What's In It For You!!!

For each person it will be different. Let me ask you this question - "If you have no outcome, reason or specific idea you want to get from this book - what are you going to get out of it?" If your answer is "Nothing", then why read this book? My goal is to give you a number of ideas that will add value to your business to make the difference you want.

I believe this book will make a difference in your personal and professional life for no other reason than "Leaders are Readers and Readers are Leaders". If you want to lead in your marketplace and set yourself apart from the rest, then read on. I know this book will give you all of the above and so much more. Please enjoy!!!

Regards,

Keith

Chapter 1 – Progress

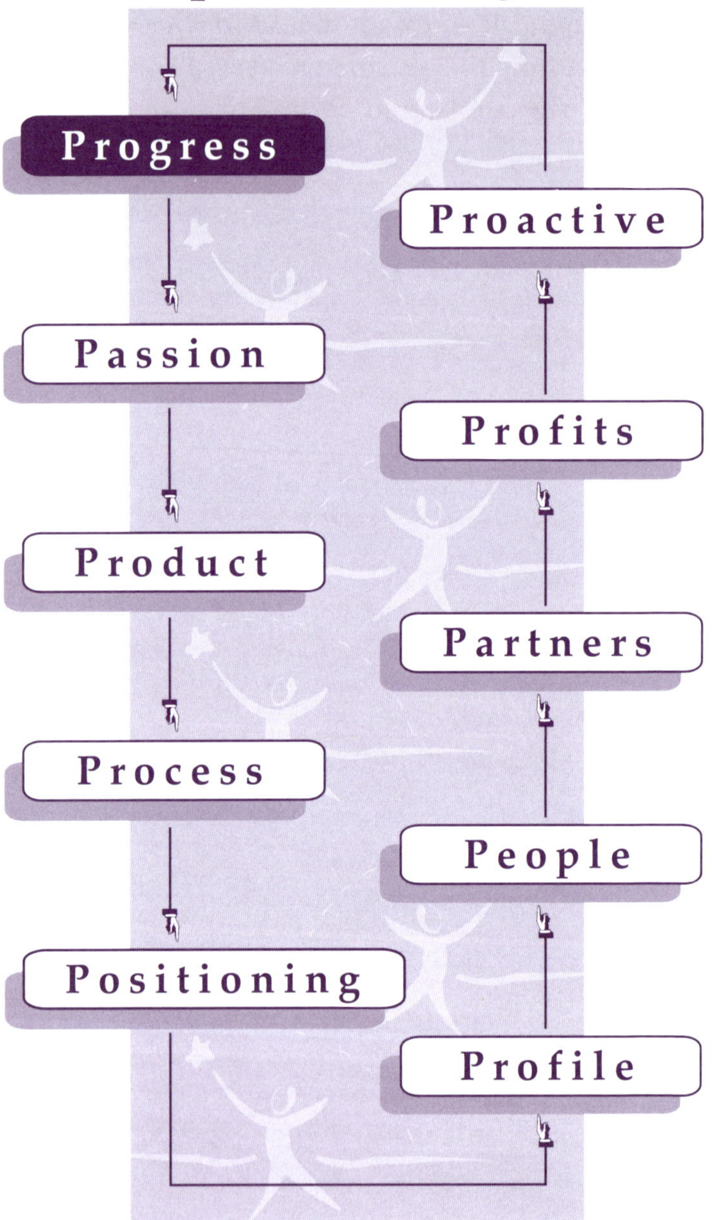

Creating Loyal Profitable Customers

PROGRESS

Change before you need to change

"Being prepared to make positive changes in your business, that's the difference between survival and significance"

When I talk to people about their businesses the one thing that comes up so often is how fast their business environment is changing. A good friend of mine once said, "We live in a fast-paced business world, where instant coffee made in a microwave is too slow. We live in an ever-changing, dynamic business world that demands us to be prepared to change."

Most people are reluctant to change; to do things differently. I believe the greatest skill you and I need for the future is the ability to adapt to our ever-changing environment, to be flexible and to have a mentality that business is about changing, before we need to change.

Remember, we will have to make changes or we will be made to change. I don't know about you, but I like to control my future by changing with the times, not waiting to be made to change because I didn't change 12 months ago. I meet people and they tell me they have had ten years' experience in their industry and I always wonder, is it ten years' experience or one year's experience repeated ten times!

Where Are You Now in Your Business?

Let's determine where you are now in your business. A change model I was introduced to is one that comes from a book called

'The Empty Raincoat' written by Charles Handy. The model is called the Sigmoid Curve. We use a modified version of this model in our business on a regular basis to assist us in determining where we are in a number of key areas.

Here is an example of the model we refer to as the "Zero to Hero" Business Review.

Where are you on this curve in your business?

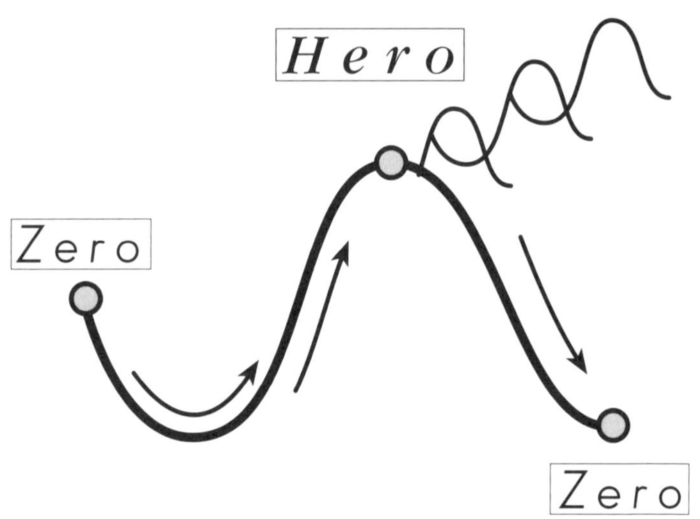

"Hero to Zero Curve"

You see, we all start off at zero when we first start out in business and, in most cases, we have a number of learning experiences that are not necessarily earning experiences. We go down the hill and then we start to master our marketplace and we work our way up to hero status in our own mind. Then, if we change, we head down to zero and that zero is normally depicted by hard times, loss of profits, customers and maybe even closure of our business. Therefore, our goal in business is to change before we achieve hero status. This means that if you make a decision today, can you implement it today?

No, it takes time and this is known as *lag* time. There is a lag in time before a result can be reaped from that decision or *change*.

I think we have all seen businesses that should have changed but they didn't because they were either in their comfort zone, or they were the market leader. They may have even become arrogant and didn't believe they needed to change because everything was going so well. You see, once we start to reach our goals, we need to be focused on the next level, the next set of goals, or our next achievement.

The question that is highlighted on the *Zero to Hero* model is relevant to a number of your key business areas. Ask yourself the question, "When it comes to my specific business areas, where am I now on this curve?"

Here are the areas to think about in your business; -

- Products and Services
- Teamwork
- Productivity of Your People
- Customer Service
- Customer Loyalty
- Profitability
- Systems and Processes
- Innovation
- Marketing and Profiling

Place a mark where you believe your business is for each one of these areas on the Zero to Hero model.

We need great vision and imagination to go to the next level in the business marketplace.

There are basically two things that stop us going to the next level in our business, once we have determined the need to change. The first is our "Vision" for what is the next level we want to achieve in our business. The second is our "Imagination" i.e. how we are going to get to that level.

Look at these famous quotes from people or organisations that kept on thinking about what the next level was in their business:

'I think there is a world market for maybe five computers.'

Thomas Watson, Chairman IBM - 1943

'640K ought to be enough memory for anybody.'

Bill Gates, Chairman Microsoft - 1981

'Computers in the future will weigh no more than 1.5 tons.'

Popular Mechanics - 1949

How to Make Change Work for You

So where do you need to change? The first thing you need to know is that, if you continually change, then change is no big deal. All you need to do is to make small changes this week that will make a difference next week, and make changes next week that will make a difference the week after. Then in 52 weeks' time you will be moving in a positive, proactive, progressive way towards your business goals.

Think about these facts: At the 1956 Melbourne Olympics Murray Rose won the gold medal in the 1500 metres men's freestyle event: In 1996 at the Atlanta Olympics, Kieren Perkins won a gold medal in the 1500 metres men's freestyle event. If these two swimmers could have raced against each other, Kieren Perkins would have beaten Murray Rose by six and a half laps. Yes, I know pools have gotten quicker, training techniques have changed, diets have improved and even Speedos have gotten a lot smaller. The point is this: the swimmers didn't say, "We are going to shave a lap off this year." They said, "Let's take off just half a second", and over a 40 year period they have whittled it down. Think about making small changes today that will make a big difference in the future.

Questions to move you through change

Here are some questions to think about when it comes to changing your business. Think of them as the "Four P's" of change.

- **Purpose** - Why do you need to change in your business or career?
- **Picture** - Where do you want your business to be in the future?
- **Plan** - How are you going to get to your future business picture?
- **Part** - What part are you and your people going to play in your change process?

In the next chapter, we will talk about your vision for your business and how to create a plan of action to reach your goals. But for now, what is the one thing you need to change in your business or career that would make a significant difference?

Now more than ever we need to be proactive in our approach within our marketplace. We need to think about our future, take action upon those thoughts and continue to look for better ways to do business: Whether it is with technology; new marketing techniques; or effective product distribution channels. Whatever it is, we need to make it happen, not just let it happen. Here are some statistics about change and making goals come true in your business:

3% of people set goals with an action plan
that relates to change.

10% of people set goals about change, but never write them down.
These people expect things to happen.

60% have vague or limited goals about change.
They watch things happen.

27% of people have no goals at all and don't change.
These people don't know what happened!
Where has life gone? What have I achieved?

Where do you see yourself?

Chapter 1 - Practical business projects

Please answer the following questions to assist you in clarifying what you need to change in your business or career.

1. Why do you need to change in the way you do business?

____

____

____

____

2. Where do you want your business or career to be in the future?

____

____

____

____

3. How are you going to get to your future business or career picture?

____

____

____

____

4. What part are you and your people going to play in your change process?

____

____

____

____

5. What is the one thing you need to change in your current business or career that would make a significant difference in the future?

____

____

____

____

Chapter 2 – Passion

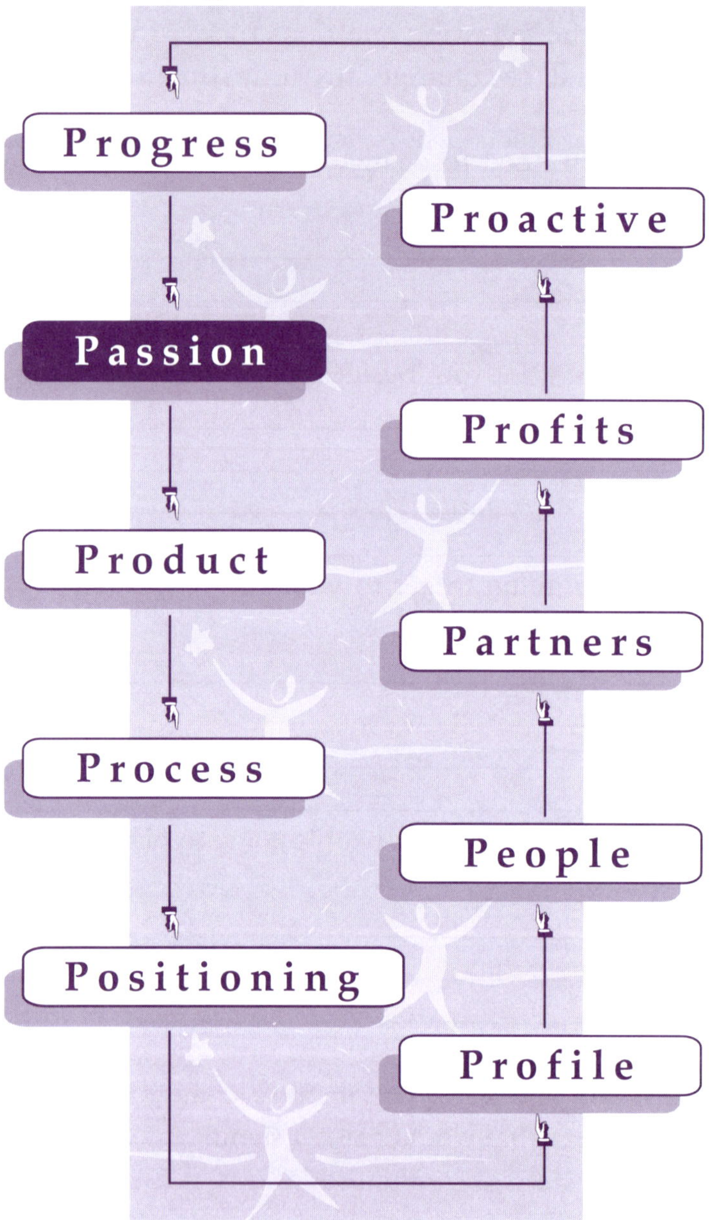

Creating Loyal Profitable Customers

PASSION

Creating a passion worth pursuing

"You will either pursue your passion, or you will live with regret forever."

Business needs to be enjoyable, not a trial, a hassle or a stress generator. You see, my philosophy is simple when it comes to business and work. Your businesses or career should be a vehicle that creates a lifestyle for yourself and your family. I also believe that you are a long time dead. So you better enjoy what you do, otherwise you will become like some people I meet. They are dead from the neck up! You know the people I mean they have lost their spirit, desire, drive and passion to live. They died years ago; we just have not buried them yet.

Life is too short to live without a passion for something. Find your passion and pursue it.

Why do you need a passion in business?

Everyone needs a passion to pursue in life and in business. I think in today's business world we sometimes lack the passion to fuel our motivation. In other words we have all become a little bit too serious for our own good. We need to have a passion in our business that lays a foundation to set us apart from our competitors.

I think there are basically three levels in business:

- **Survival,** where you just get by but you don't get ahead. I think we all know people in this category who are just hoping to make it through this month, this quarter or this year.
- **Success,** where you have been making progress, but you realise that it is now time to change and go to the next level in your market place
- **Significant,** where you are recognised as the industry leader by your customers and competitors.

There are basically three levels in business. Survival - Success - Significant. Which level describes your business at the moment?

There are great rewards for being significant in your market place which range from: being top of mind with your customers; having good people want to work for you and; attracting endless referrals to your business. If you don't read any further, the question you must answer for yourself is, "How do I become significant in my marketplace?" Because, if you are not significant in your market place, then why should people do business with you?

At the end of this chapter there are more questions for you to think about and work through. As you may have realised good service is no longer good enough. Your market place has become better educated, more astute. It has more choices than ever before, which makes it more demanding.

Good service is no longer good enough in today's marketplace.

My philosophy, when it comes to business these days you need to have a passion that drives you, otherwise you will be lost in the battle. Whether you are in business for yourself or work for someone else, your goals and motivation are generated by your passion to achieve a certain outcome. This outcome, or your passion, is the cornerstone for what you do now and your lighthouse for your future.

You see, without a passion for your business it makes it difficult to have a positive influence with your people, enough to create long-term customer loyalty. Remember, everyone needs a reason to go the extra mile to create customer loyalty in your business.

Creating your business passion model for business

Let's talk about how to create a passion for business. The model displayed below is something we have designed for our business. It has made a great difference to how we look at our business and what we do on a regular basis to remain focused on what counts.

The formula is about clarifying your long term vision and goals then looking at the specific strategy to make your goals come true. You need to make sure you have the right business to transport you toward your goals. Now if you have this formula in place you have a greater chance of obtaining significant success in your personal and professional life.

Goal Setting Formula

÷ Strategy x Business Vehicle

=

Significant Success

Vision for your business success

The first part of this model involves determining your vision for your business.

I remember reading a story about Walt Disney. It told of how, after he had built Disneyland in California, he took a trip to Orlando Florida and as he looked around the area, he thought that it would be a perfect spot for Walt Disney World. Prior to this amusement park ever being opened he passed away, but the construction and his vision lived on. On the opening day of Walt Disney World, his brother Roy Disney was asked to escort the media through the park. As he did so, one of the journalists made the off-handed comment, "Isn't it a shame that Walt never saw this place open?" Roy Disney replied, "He did! He just happened to see it first in his mind, before you and I saw it today."

You have got to see what you want to achieve in your mind, before you will ever have it in reality - *VISION.*

Here are some questions to get you thinking about your businesses future.

- What is it that you want to achieve in your business?
- What is it that you want to achieve in your life?
- Where do you see your business or career in 12 months' time?
- Where do your see your business in 5 years' time?
- What do you want to create in your marketplace with your business?
- If you created a business that people considered to be significant, what would it look like?

You need to know where you are going, because if you don't stand for something, you will fall for anything.

The first key to your success, when discussing a customer loyalty foundation, is to have a desire to create a business that is built on customer loyalty. Customer loyalty will be the key to your long-term business success in the future. You will not be measured on turnover alone, but you will be measured on the loyalty of your customer base: how many times they buy from you: how often they buy from you: where your customers come from: what their preferences are and how much information you have captured about them.

Strategy for success

It is much easier approach if you break your vision down into the parts that make up your business. People who have vague goals, get vague results. This step is about assisting you to clarify your specific milestones, targets and outcomes.

Now we all know people who are going to do this or that and people that should have done this or should have done that. You have got to be careful that you don't should all over yourself. By taking your vision and creating a plan built upon action you are taking yourself out of this "should have" category. Once you have determined your vision for the future it is time to clarify your goals and develop a plan of action to make them come true.

Firstly, here are some areas to think about when you break your vision down into a specific plan. These are just some generic business areas to get your planning process started in your business.

Key performance business areas

- Products - Have I got the right products for the markets I want to compete in?
- Profits - How much money do I want to make and what is my profit to expenditure ratio?
- Profile - What do I need to do to market my business, my products and myself so that they are of the highest profile in the markets I want to compete in?
- Positioning - What type of customers and business do I want to attract to my business?
- Processes - What systems do I need to put into place so that my business runs smoothly with, or even, without me?
- Professional Growth - What skills, knowledge and techniques do I need to improve if I am going to take my business or career to the next level?

- People - What type of people do I need to employ to be able to reach these goals? How many people do I need? What skills do they need? Where will I find them?
- Performance - What are the key performance indicators I am going to measure and focus on in my business? How many customers do I need? How much money will they spend with me?

To help you put your strategies into a specific structure here is a visual model that I use with businesses when we are formulating their long-term strategic plan.

Work your way through these boxes. Determine the areas that make up your business. Then identify the milestones you want to achieve and clarify your deadlines for when you want these strategies to be completed.

Business vehicle to drive your success

Your business or career is the vehicle that can take you where you want to go. Have you got the right business vehicle to help you achieve these professional and personal goals? Whether your goals relate to your personal or professional direction, your business is a vehicle to help you reach your desired outcomes. Remember, life is a journey and to travel on this journey you need a vehicle.

The good part about the means of transport is that you have a choice in how you want to travel.

Significant success achievement

This is how people will describe your business as you achieve your key goals and specific outcomes.This is my definition of significant success - Doing what you love to do, being rewarded with not only an outstanding income, but also by peer and marketplace recognition. Here is a good exercise for you to consider right now.Think about what significant success means to you? Complete the following Practical business project.

Significant success - Doing what you love to do, being rewarded with not only an outstanding income, but also by peer and market place recognition.

From time to time the business world has a habit of throwing up challenges in front of us. It is only when we have a clearly defined vision, with a plan built upon action, that we can see through these challenges, or roadblocks, to our final destination.This is why it is vital for both you and I to have a vision where we want to take our businesses and ourselves in the future.

Chapter 2 - Practical business projects

Please answer the following questions to assist you in clarifying your business vision and your passion for being in business.

1. What can you do to become significant in your market place?

2. What is it that you want to achieve in your life and in business?

3. Where do you see yourself in twelve months' time?

4. Where do you see yourself in five years' time?

5. What do you want to create in your marketplace with your business?

6. If you created a business that people considered to be significant, what would it look like?

7. What does significant success mean to you?

Chapter 3 – Product

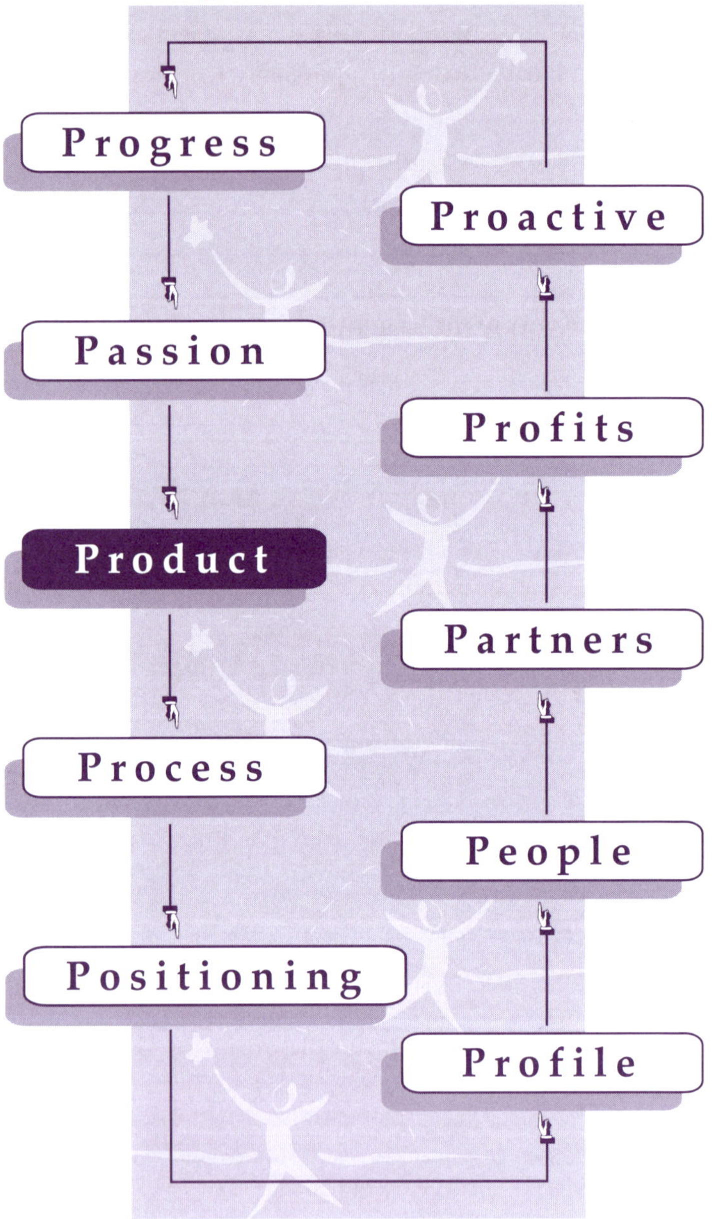

Creating Loyal Profitable Customers

PRODUCT

What business are you really in?

"Regardless of what product or service we sell, we are in the business of creating a customer service experience that people will rave about forever."

Creating the right service selling experience for your customers

Every business has a product or service to provide to their marketplace. The challenge we face in business is - does the marketplace want or need our product? People get very excited about a new product that is going to do fantastic things and believe that customers are going to beat a path to their doorway from near and far to buy it. They think it's going to be great and they are going to make money from it. The problem is they sometimes get so worked up about the product they forget to give the customer the experience that goes with the product.

A service selling experience is based on the philosophy that the more you serve the more you will sell, the more happy customers you have the more people will be referred to your business. In other words, you create such an experience for the customer that they are not only delighted, but also become an advocate for your business.

Let me ask you, can you recall a time when you bought a product that you were very happy with, but the service experience or the buying experience left a bad taste in your mouth? Most likely your answer is "Yes!" I don't understand why people get confused about this issue of creating a positive purchasing experience for their customers. Products or marketing programs don't sell products. People sell products when they create a service experience that their customers say "That was nice" or "Wow, great service".

Remember - Anybody can sell anything once, but if you want to make the second, third and fourth sale, you must create a positive service experience that people will rave about forever.

Do you sell a physical or memorable product?

What are you really selling or what do your customers really buy from you? I think we have all heard the story about the home handyman who goes to the hardware store to buy a drill. Is he really buying a drill, or is he buying a hole in the wall? He just needs the drill to get the hole in the wall. People buy solutions and experiences that are generated by your business. We need to give people, both a physical product and a memorable experience.

In the past you could be very successful by just providing a great physical product. Now we have to not only provide a great product, but we also need to provide a memorable experience to support this total buying solution.

I remember that when we bought our first BMW from Brisbane BMW it was a memorable experience. Every other time I bought a car I purchased a physical product, just another car. When we bought this car it was an experience from the moment we met the salesman for the first time, to the day we picked up the car, to the thank you a week later and the personal phone call ten days after we had the car, to our first service. They kept on creating an experience to support the physical product and that's how you become memorable.

Product flogger vs. problem solver

There are two types of salespeople in the marketplace. People who just go out and sell a product, then look for the next prospect to sell their product to, are commonly known as "Product Floggers". They find, flog and forget you. They sell to their needs not yours. They are only concerned with their goals, their targets and their wallet. They provide little or no service and often have a mentality of "Who is going to be my next sale"?

Here are some of the characteristics of a Product Flogger:

- They are not interested in your needs or the outcomes you want to achieve.
- They have a "next" mentality or, in other words, they want to sell you something so they can get on with selling to the next person.
- They are an "order taker", not a solution provider.
- They don't listen to you to understand your specific needs.
- They don't try to build trust, credibility or rapport with you.
- They are not looking for a long-term relationship.

The following diagram demonstrates where they spend most of their time.

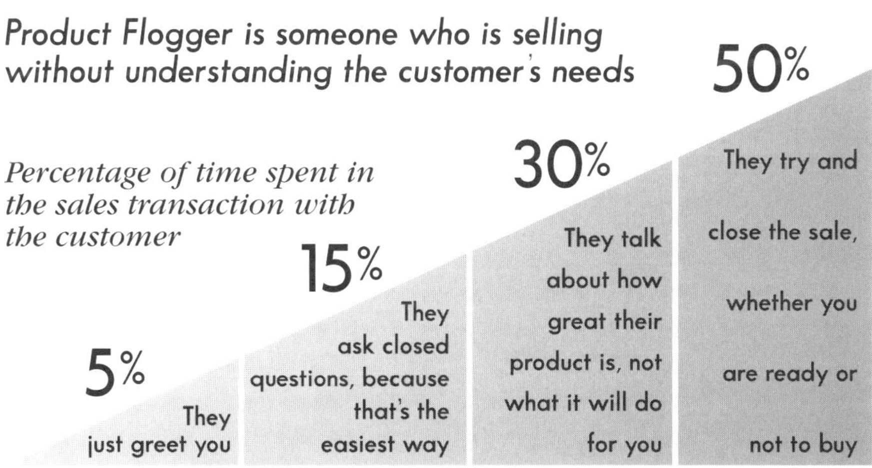

In essence, the Problem Solver bridges the gap between where the customer is currently, to what the customer wants to achieve in the future. They do this by providing a solution, using their products or services based on customers' needs.

Here are some of the characteristics of a Problem Solver.

- They seek to provide solutions to their customer's needs.
- They identify what the customer's key outcomes are by asking questions.
- They want a long-term relationship with the customer.
- They improve themselves so that their expertise is considered an asset by the customer.
- They are honest in all their dealings and they often recommend products they don't stock to solve the customer's problems.
- They tell the customer how they will benefit from their product, not just about the features of the product.

The following diagram demonstrates where the Problem Solver spends their time with a customer.

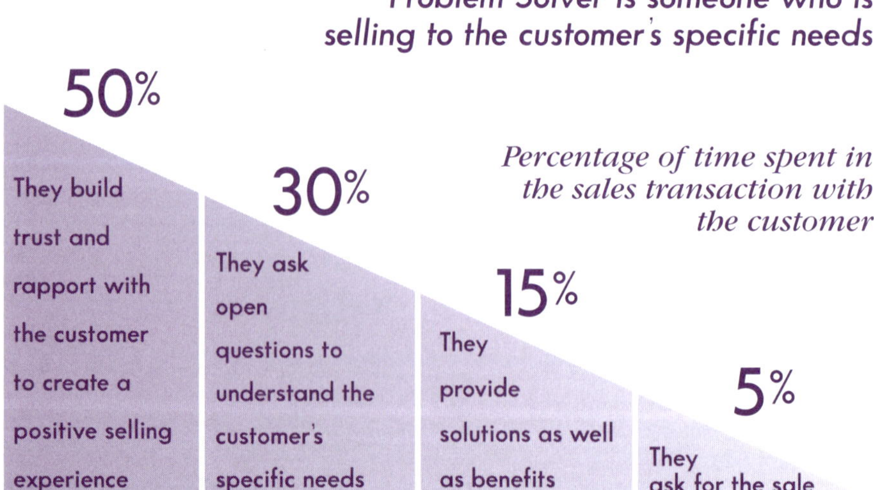

Your physical product

Let's look at exactly what your physical product is in your business. Your physical product is what your customers walk out the door with or the service they are now benefitting from. Here are some key questions to ask yourself and your people. Who knows, your people may not be aware of what you are really selling in your business.

- What are your core products or services?
- What real solutions do you sell to your customers?
- Are your products still desired by your target market?
- How long will that desire last before you have to replace that product or service?
- If you were to replace it, what type of product do you think it would be replaced with?
- What other products could you introduce to your marketplace which would complement your existing range of products or services?

Products come and go, but the service selling experience can last forever.

Your memorable product

This part of your sales experience is about creating an experience for the customer that they will long remember and tell their friends and associates about. It needs to be an exceptional service selling experience. Anyone can sell something once, but the service experience will give people a reason to return time and time again. Nobody likes going to the dentist and I was the president of that club until some friends of ours referred us to my current dentist at the A.J.Medland Centre in Brisbane. They create an experience for you every time you go there and it's a great experience: from the moment they greet you by name at the front door; to your favourite selection of music playing while your teeth are checked out; to when they introduce you around to every staff member including Mr. Tony Medland the owner; to the personal phone call a day after your visit from the dental assistant to make sure everything is O.K.; to the hand written note from the dentist who treats you. My wife had some rather painful root canal work done. After it was all finished and, as she was leaving, they gave her a bunch of flowers to thank her for being so brave.

The price your customer paid will be long forgotten, but the quality of your service will be remembered forever.

The 5 basic reasons why people don't buy from you

There are all types of reasons why people don't buy from you. Here are five reasons to think about when creating an experience for your customers:

1. Credibility - They don't like you. Maybe you have not built enough trust or a high level of credibility with your customer.
2. Need - They don't need your product. You are selling drills and they have all the holes they need.
3. Understanding - They don't understand what your product can do for them. The customer is unsure of what you are actually selling or how it could save them time, money or effort.
4. Value - They don't see the value of your product. People will pay extra for a product, if they believe in their own mind it is of value to them.
5. Invited - They are not invited to purchase your product. We sometimes educate our customers to buy from our competitors because we don't ask the simple question, "Would you like to take that one?" Instead we let them walk out the door.

So where does price come into the five reasons? It comes primarily into number four. If people don't think something is of value then they say it is too expensive, because they cannot see how it adds value to them or how it solves their problem. By the way, people do say your product or service is too expensive when they don't like you as in number one, because that becomes an easier option to explain.

Identify which one of these five is the reason why people don't buy from you from time to time. Then identify how you are going to improve it. When you take away the reasons why people don't buy from you, you can stand back and watch your business grow. In our business we have a little saying "We will get them all!" Because we are prepared to stay in touch with people long enough, we are going to take every excuse away from them for not doing business with us. We are going to add value to them or their business before they do business with us. In other words we are going to wear people down in the nicest possible way.

Think about it this way. 60% of sales people give up after the first "No", and 95% of sales people have given up after the sixth "No". You do need to be tenacious but your opportunity of success increases in this prospecting process as you continue to add value to your customer.

4 Strategic Ways to Grow Your Business

All businesses are different, but there are four ways to grow your business. We often do a few things very well but we let the others slide. When you combine all four, it has a profound effect on your business. I call it the "Multiplying Factor". It is almost as good as compounding interest. Here are the four ways; -

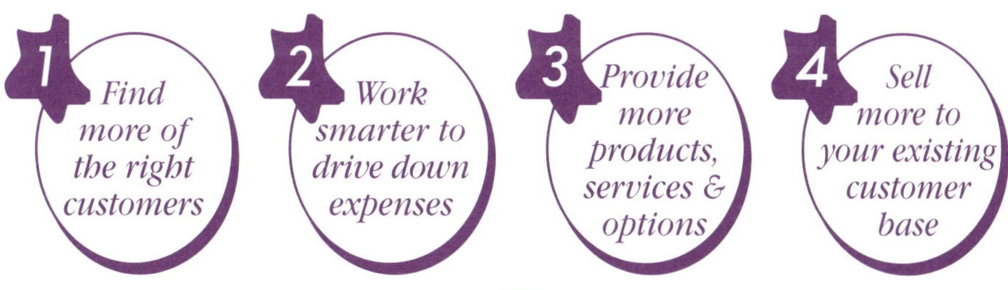

1. Find More of The Right Customers

Traditionally in business this is what we have all done. Creating and growing our businesses through advertising, asking for referrals, mail outs, special introductory offers, open invitations to visit our store or through cold calling of prospective customers. The only challenge is that we get all types of customers. I think we have all heard the phrase "The customer is always right". What a load of garbage! Let me rephrase it for you, "The right customer is always right". Not every customer is right for your business. Not every customer is going to appreciate your services or expertise, so go and find the ones that will. Give the dud customers to your competitors and let them have the hassles.

The customer is not always right; but the right customer is always right.

Another way to look at identifying your perfect customer is by looking at your existing customer base and developing a profile of your top 20% most profitable customers. I think we are all familiar with the 80/20 rule, that is, 80% of your income will come from 20% of your customers. To see if this is true for your business look at your top 20% of customers and work out how much income they give you. If you have not done this before, it is a great exercise to do.

Identify what the perfect customer is for your business. Ask yourself these simple questions before you go out looking for new customers:

- What does a perfect customer look like?
- Where do you find them?
- How many products or services should they, or could they, be using of yours?
- How many referrals do they give you in a year?
- What is the best way to contact them?

- What advertising would appeal to them the most?
- What level of service would they appreciate?
- How do they like to do business?
- What motivates them to buy your products and services?
- What sales approach or offers would appeal to them the best?

When you try to become a master to many, you become a slave to none.

2. Working smarter to drive down expenses

At the end of the day if you have all these great customers buying lots of products, but you don't make a profit, why are you in business? I have seen businesses that have a great turnover but could not make a profit. Working smarter is about looking at ways to run your business more effectively. Not long ago I read Bill Gates' book - 'Business at the Speed of Thought.' There is a great chapter called the 'Paperless Office.' As you and I know this concept has been flirted with since the 1980's. It is only now that we have the technology to fully appreciate how to implement it. After reading this chapter it inspired me to find ways to make our business run more effectively by using technology and the resources currently available. More on this in Chapter 9 - Profits.

3. Providing more products, services and options

Your customers are buying a product to solve a problem or to meet a need. Sometimes you need to look at the products you currently sell and review if they are still needed or are still in demand. This requires a cold hard look at reality. What does your customer want, not what do you want to sell? You then need to take a look at what other products or services add value to your existing product range that would complement what you are currently doing. Now before you get carried way with having to extend your ever increasing product range, these products or services may not be yours, they could be businesses that you have set up a strategic alliance with or with suitable financial remuneration program. Once again, ask yourself the following questions to clarify what additional product or service opportunities exist in your marketplace.

- What other products or services would add value to our existing range of products or services?
- Who could we team up with to provide a greater level of service or some additional products?
- What other services or products would complement our existing products and service?
- What products will we need to develop or source in future for us to be competitive in our marketplace?

4. Selling more to our existing customers

The only way you are going to sell more to your existing customers is by having a relationship that adds value to them, their business or enhances their lifestyle. In doing this you create real customer loyalty. Customers return to businesses that give them a reason to return. In the following chapters I will give you a number of strategies to ensure that your customers keep on coming back to your business.

*In the future **customer loyalty** will be king in the worldwide business environment we compete in.*

Chapter 3 - Practical business projects

Please answer the following questions to assist you in clarifying what your product focus should be in the future.

1. Why don't more people buy your products or services?

2. What could you do to overcome these reasons in the future?

3. What level of service would your customers like to receive from you?

4. What does the perfect customer look like for your business?

5. What other products or services would add value to your existing range of products or services?

Chapter 4 – Process

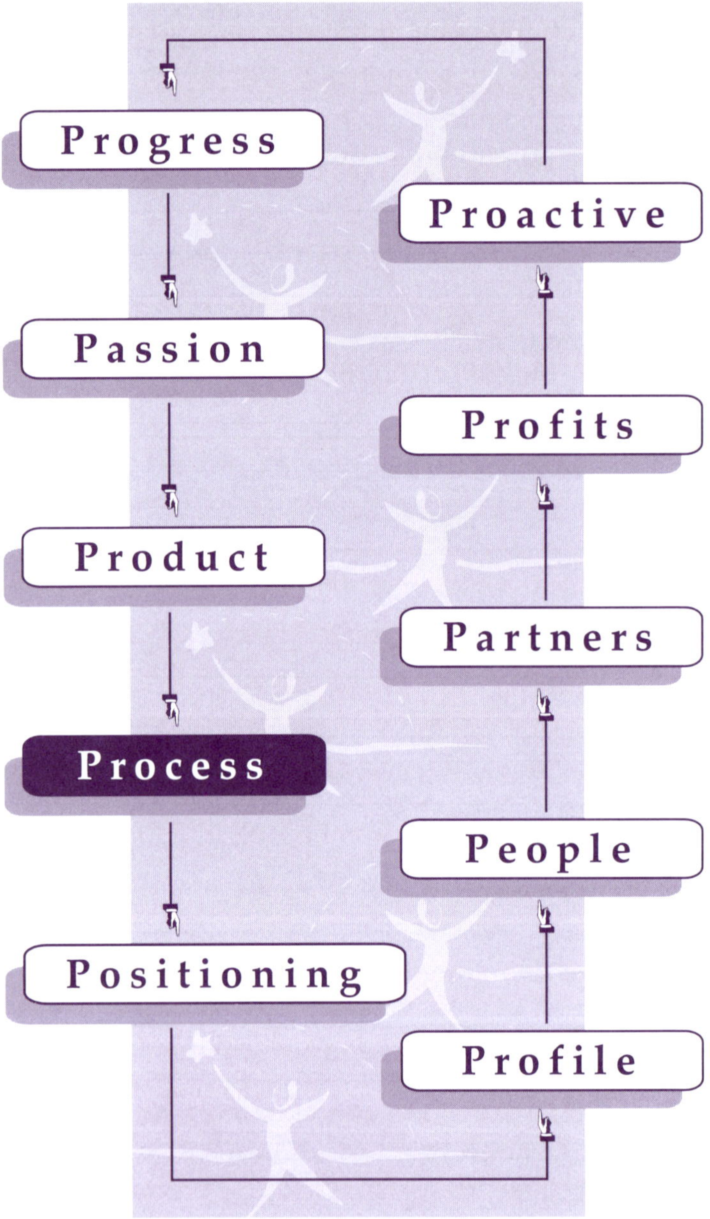

Creating Loyal Profitable Customers

PROCESS

Creating a service selling system with personality

"Systems drive businesses and people drive the systems that create an experience, so that customers come back time and time again."

Consistency is the key to building a great business which lasts the test of time.This consistency comes from a system that lets you reproduce the same results over and over again. In this chapter I would like to explore the key elements you need to have in place to make customer loyalty work in your business.To create a service selling system that works, you need to integrate the technology processes with your service processes.

A service selling system is a system where selling becomes the result of the service experience that is consistently given to your customers.This selling system is where you can have the greatest impact in your business when building customer loyalty. But remember the goal of the process is to create a service selling experience. Don't lose sight of this goal by focussing so much on the process that you forget about the customer, as so often happens with totally automated businesses.

Benefits of creating a service selling system for your business

When you create your service selling system the benefits are many. There are three benefits that I believe will have the greatest impact. They are: firstly, that your business becomes easier to walk away from if you want to devote more time to other interests, secondly, your business becomes easier to up skill your team members to operate it, so you can develop other opportunities and; thirdly it makes your business more saleable when it comes time to move on to something else in your personal and professional life.

Look at it this way. If you were looking at two businesses to purchase, which one would you choose? One of them has little or no systems in place, no customer database and none of the processes that has made that business work in the past. The second business has a well-organised customer database with the purchasing habits recorded, every process of the business recorded and there are systems in place that make sense and are giving the customer a great level of service.

Which one would you buy? Where would you invest your time and money?

The service selling experience that makes a difference

Remember if someone has a great product, it is only a matter of time before someone else will duplicate it or improve upon it. So we must ask ourselves, "What can we do to differentiate ourselves in the service selling experience?" Your people and your processes create this experience. The service selling experience is made up of four parts. These are: the actions we take before the sale is made: during the selling process: after the sale is made and: long after the sale was made. We need all processes in place to create customer loyalty, as the following model displays.

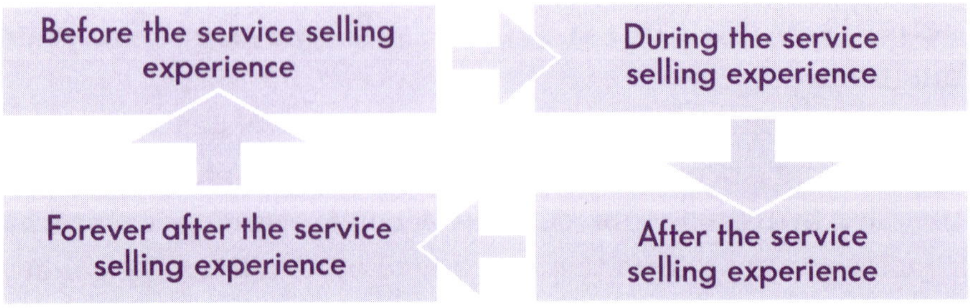

Before the service selling experience → During the service selling experience

↓

After the service selling experience → Forever after the service selling experience

↑ (back to Before the service selling experience)

Before the service selling experience - a reason to enter your business

In any sales service process, giving the customer the reason to enter is critical. We often overlook the things we can do to prepare ourselves, and our people for the pending customer interaction and possible sales transaction.

Have you given your customers enough reasons to enter your business? Whether they physically have to walk through a shop door or pick up a phone to contact you, have you given them enough reasons to make the effort?

How many times have you seen an advertisement or special offer that has caught your attention, then when you visited the store or called up to inquire, the service was ordinary or the staff were not aware of the offer or it was just a poor experience?

Why go and spend the money there in the first place?

Let's look at all the aspects to consider before your business opens for trading today:

1. Are you using the right marketing tools to draw people to your business?
2. Have you developed the customer service and selling skills of your people?
3. Does everyone know the customer service standards you follow?
4. Have you spent time developing everyone's product knowledge?
5. Is your product displayed in the most appealing manner?
6. Have you documented all the processes that make up your service selling experience?

7. Have you given your existing customers a real reason to return to your business with a compelling offer?
8. Have you streamlined your business so that it is easy to do business with you from the customer's point of view?
9. Does each department know what the other departments do in your business?
10. Do departments and people within those departments work together or against one another?
11. Are your people presenting themselves and the image of your business in the best possible way?
12. Have you put a loyalty gaining system in place for your business?
13. Have you got a continuous flow of referrals coming into your business?
14. Does everyone know your business goals and have their own professional and personal goals for the week or month ahead?
15. Have you empowered your people so that they can make decisions?
16. Have your people been trained in the proper telephone skills?

Look at all of these aspects before your business opens for trading today.

I like that quote "Prior planning prevents poor performance".To do that, lay a strong foundation to build your service selling experience on and you will give your customers a reason to enter into a business relationship with you.

During the service selling experience - a reason to purchase from your business

So now that the customer has entered your business, you can start to create a service selling experience for them whether they buy anything from you or not. Your goal is, you want them to make a purchase, but if they don't buy anything from you, you want to give them a great experience so they will come back the next time to make a purchase.

This part of the service selling experience can be divided into four components;-

The Service Selling experience

1. Relationship building

This is where you take the opportunity to build rapport, trust and credibility with your customers. First impressions are lasting ones, starting from what you say to them when you first meet. It's about how you greet the customer. It may be as simple as saying "Can I help you?" and you know that the potential customer is just looking. You may want to say, "I know that you are just looking. My name is ...., if I can be of any assistance I will be over there."

You see, service selling is about creating a positive impression relating to each customer, meeting them at their level and having the attitude that you want to serve the customer, not avoid them. It's about being approachable and flexible in your environment.

Here are ten things that you can do to build the relationship with your customers.

1. Use your customer's name.
2. Be honest in your dealings with your customers.
3. Pay total attention and focus on the customer.
4. Let the customer know each step along the way what is happening.
5. Make agreements, keep those agreements and follow up on the customer.
6. Use professional telephone skills, if you put them on hold, keep them posted.
7. Be a good listener, listen for the underlying messages, then paraphrase to confirm your customer's needs.
8. Don't use jargon with your customer.
9. Make sure your store, your product and your personal presentation is professional.
10. Have great product knowledge. Know what you are talking about.

2. Identifying needs

The customer has basically 2 needs, a known need and an unknown need. A known need is when the customer knows what they want and they tell you. An unknown need is where the customer does not know what they want. By asking open quality questions starting with Who; When; Where; Why; What and How, you move them from the unknown to the known. You can then determine the specific needs of the customer so that you can recommend the right product or service to meet those needs.

What questions could you ask your customers to build the relationship, understand their needs, give the customer a unique and enjoyable experience and create that point of difference? Have you ever thought about the questions you and your people ask? Do your people ask any questions at all, or do they get into telling the customer how great your product or service is?

I always think about the parallels between an amateur golfer and the professional salesperson. The amateur golfer turns up, goes to the first tee and tees off. The ball is lost or not that far away after teeing off. The amateur service selling person is similar. They just turn up and wait for someone to buy something from them through no skill of their own. The difference in this scenario is, at least in golf, you get a second chance if you stuff up the first shot, unlike your customers. The professional golfer, on the other hand, practises all week; they hit thousands of golf balls from different hazards, angles and positions. They turn up early on match day, practise their putting, warm up and go to the first tee ready to play. The professional service selling person thinks about their business, customers and opportunities. They develop strategies and plan their questions to obtain the best possible results. Are you and your people amateurs or professionals?

Always remember, he or she who asks the questions is always in control. Get good at asking questions. The more you understand where your customers are going, the challenges they face, what they want to achieve, the quicker you will be able to provide a real solution and be of value to them.

Here are some basic questions you can ask to not only determine their needs, but also their background, goals, buying motivators and previous experiences with your type of product or service.

Quality questions to determine your customer's needs

- ***What are your business goals in the short term or long term?***
- ***What are the major challenges you currently face in your business?***
- ***Tell me about your business, your products and the services you provide?***
- ***Who are some of your major competitors in your marketplace?***
- ***What do they do differently from you?***
- ***Who are the key decision makers in your business?***
- ***What have been some of your major achievements in the past 12 months and some of your setbacks?***
- ***What do you do well in your business?***
- ***What would you like to improve in your business?***
- ***What are some of the strategies you have planned to make these improvements happen?***
- ***Tell me about your people. How would you describe your team to me: skills: abilities: individual needs: level of experience.***
- ***What are the areas of potential you would like these people to be able to tap into in the future?***
- ***What's most important to you when you make an investment in a product/service like mine?***

- ***What has to happen to make you feel you have received that?***
- ***How do you normally market your products and services?***
- ***What have you done in the past to gain greater customer loyalty?***
- ***Do you have the following in place in your business:***

Regular Team Meetings	***Business Planning***	***Loyalty Program***
Marketing Plan	***Regular Client Contact***	***Database***
Ask & Get Referrals	***Customers Classified***	***Sales Process***

The type of questions and amount of questions will vary with the type of environment you sell in. If you are someone selling a consumable product over the counter or the telephone you may only have the opportunity to ask a few questions, but if you are selling a total IT solution to a major company, the needs analysis process could be quite long. You may want to think about the questions that apply to your business and design your own needs analysis form to use in your business.

3. Providing a solution

Now that you know your customer's needs, your role is to provide an appropriate solution to meet these needs. This involves explaining your product and services in a way that relates to the customer's needs and level of understanding. In other words show the customer how your product will solve their challenge. This is not the time to be talking about all the features of your product. It is about relating to the customer the specific benefits that will be of interest to that customer in light of what they have told you about their situation and circumstances.

When you talk about the features of the product, the customers think to themselves, "So what will it really do for me?" When you share the product benefits, they think to themselves "So how does it really help me?" When you relate the ***exact*** benefits to the specific customer's needs they think to themselves, "Now I know how it helps me specifically". This is when the real value of your solutions has its full impact with your customers. Anybody can talk about features and benefits, but the skilled professional is able to make them relate to each customer.

4. Decision making

Now all the customer has to do is make a decision. Your involvement in this process is to help them make that decision. It could be answering any additional questions, handling an objection, discussing payment options, giving them a follow-up call or by simply asking for the sale. Some of your customers will want to think about it, some will be very decisive, some will want to do more research and some will need you to make a decision for them.

Your role is to support and guide them in the most appropriate way. You may need to improve on how to handle your most common objections or how to ask for the sale. By carrying out the three parts of the service selling experience mentioned above you will achieve a much higher level of success.

After the service selling experience - reasons to recommend your business

If you go and see a great movie or eat at a fabulous restaurant, how many people do you tell in the next week? Maybe five or ten people? Why do you and I do that? I think it is because of the experiences we had which was worth recommending to friends and associates. What we need to do, is not only delight our customers when they do business with us, but surprise them after the sale.

It could be as simple as a follow-up call a week later to make sure everything is O.K. It could be a personal note saying thank you for their business or for that small box of lollies you delivered with their initial purchase.

It's what you do after the sale is completed that makes the pleasant difference. It may be making sure that all the loose ends are cleaned up, correct paperwork completed, delivery times confirmed, warranty cards sent away or their correct details captured on the database. It is most important that you don't drop the ball, once you have gotten over the line with the sale.

Forever after the service selling experience - reason to return to your business

What we do after the sale is important, but what we do forever after that is critical in building long-term customer relationships and ongoing customer loyalty. Your initial service selling experience will last anywhere from a day to two weeks before the customer forgets who you are and what you did for them. Setting up your own customer loyalty schedule will keep you at the top of your customer's mind. It will remind them to return to your business when the need arises again.

Marketing gurus tell us that if you are not in touch with your customers every six weeks, they are not your customers. They may be on your database, but they are not your customers. They are just waiting to be lured away by one of your competitor's offers. One of the ways to combat this is to set up your customer loyalty system in order to stay in touch with your customers on a regular contact cycle, that is every 30, 60 or 90 days. Frequency of interaction creates a top-of-mind presence with your customers.

Often I have people say in seminars, "I contact my customers monthly and I don't seem to have too much customer loyalty."

"How do you contact them?" is my normal question and the response is, "We send out a monthly invoice and we contact them to see when they are going to pay."

The interaction must be of value. Now if your business is one where you see your customers daily or three times a week, you will need to use other means of contact to add value.

Identify where you need to improve your service selling process

Let's take a look at the service selling processes you have in place in your business. Take some time to map out every step of your service selling process from the moment a customer contacts you, to the time they get their first newsletter from your business. Look at every step along the way, every time you interface with your customers whether by phone, letter, face-to-face, fax or e-mail. Then identify how to make that process better, faster, more effective, efficient or easier to use.

Take away the roadblocks that stop your customers doing business with you or the roadblocks that stop your people from giving a great service experience.

A great way to start is to do what Federal Express (or FedEx as they are more popularly known,) did when they first got started. They asked the question, "What would give us a unique point of difference?" Someone said, "Getting a package from point A to point B, absolutely positively guaranteed to get there overnight". Then they worked backwards. How would they do it? What would they need to do?

In our business this process has been a powerful contributor in making us more consistent with the level of customer service that we provide. Our service selling system is made up of 16 steps. We know when we don't win a proposal or, if we ever drop the ball when it comes to delivering on our agreements, we can pinpoint the exact process that let us down and fix it.

Quickly, let me share an example of how it helped us last year with a challenge that was re-occurring in our business.

Once the customer decided they wanted us to work with them, we would conduct a needs analysis with our customer to gain a greater understanding of their specific conference speaker needs. This was done either as a teleconference or in a face-to-face meeting. From this meeting, I would go away and put together a proposal which we would send back to our customer.

I would then give a follow-up call four to five days after the proposal had been sent.This process would normally involve some telephone tag for one or two days.Then I would finally get in touch with the customer to check if they got the proposal. Normally they would not have had a chance to read it. I told them that was O.K. because I only called to find out whether they had received it.Then I would find out when they would like me to call them back to discuss the proposal further.They usually said to contact them in a week's time. I would diarise the date for a follow-up call.Then I would call them back to see if they had read the proposal.This was, once again, after I played telephone tag for two to three days. Finally, I would get in touch with them.They said that they had read it, but they would like to think about it a little longer or talk about the proposal.At this stage I would then find out when they wanted me to contact them again, perhaps in two weeks time.

Diarise the date, call back, play telephone tag, you know the story. At this point in time it may be five to six weeks since our first meeting.A lot of things happen in business in six weeks and what I was finding was that quite a number of proposals (including ours) were put on the back burner behind now higher priorities in their business. So we looked at our system and we identified that this was a time wasting problem that affected our conversion rate from proposal to program. We asked ourselves "How do we improve the system?"

This is what we came up with which has turned our six-week wait into a one-week answer with a 90 % conversion rate. Now we send the proposal with a small box of Whitmans chocolates that cost us less than $1.50 which turns the letter into a package and I put a "P.S." on the letter saying, "By the time it takes you to eat these chocolates, you will have read your proposal". It is so simple to fix a challenge if you can pinpoint the exact spot to fix. This is why it is vital for you to map out each step of your service selling process.

Here is a sample of a service selling system for people in a direct selling environment.

Flow chart of a service selling system - direct selling

- **Gaining prospective lead**
  Database; Referrals; Personal Contact; Direct Mail; Telemarketing List

- **Phone call to prospect**
  Contact the lead - Follow the sales track script. Your goal is to gain approval to send an information kit; or to find out to whom the appropriate person is to speak. Obtain the correct address; e-mail numbers; phone; fax and postal address.

- **Database entry**
  This can be done during the phone call, after the call or placed in the database file for input later.

- **Information kit sent out**
  In the next one to two days, we send the information kit to the future customer. A follow-up call is logged in the appropriate person's diary

to contact the prospect in five working days. Information letter; company profile; testimonials; services; customer list; business card; additional interesting information are sent out.

- **Follow-up phone call to the prospect**
  Make contact with the prospect in the next five working days, follow the sales track script. The goal of this call is to arrange an appointment with the prospect to assess their needs.

- **Customer appointment**
  The goal of this appointment is to build trust and rapport, understand the customer's needs and to find a solution to their needs. It is also to get their permission to provide them with a proposal and set a date to touch base with them again.

- **Thank-you note**
  This is written the day of the meeting and sent the next day.

- **Proposal Completed**
  The proposal is completed in the next two to four days and sent via post to the customer. A contact date is noted in your diary. Add them to the proposal pending list sheet. The proposal is sent with a wrapped box of chocolates.

- **Follow-up phone call**
  The prospect is contacted four to five days after the proposal is sent. They are asked a series of open questions to determine their interest level. An appointment may need to be made to clarify the proposal details. The goal of this call or meeting is to integrate the program into their business.

- **Pre-program meeting**
  This could be over the phone or face-to-face prior to starting the work. Pre-program questions answered.

- **Work completed**
  The job is completed and feedback is gained on the customer's level of satisfaction.

- **Thank-you note and gift is sent**
  This is done the day after the job is completed.

- **Follow-up call - asking for testimonial**
  The customer is contacted three to five days after the successful product delivery to ask for a verbal testimonial. Check if they got the gift and invoice. Also mention that you will call them in a week to ask for referrals. The follow-up date is placed in the diary.

- **Follow-up call to ask for referrals**
  One week after the testimonial contact the customer to get three to five referrals. Ask the customer to contact the referrals and mention that you will be calling them. Put it into the diary to contact them as a general 'how's things going call' for 30 days' time.

- **Thank-you note and gift for referrals**
  Once the referral has been contacted and a result obtained, the referee (the customer) is written a thank-you note and a small gift.

- **Four-week follow-up call**
  Four weeks from the last point of contact the customer is contacted to see how everything is going and to check on the product and to gain some valuable feedback about achievements.

Database loyalty program

This customer is classified and put into a loyalty program which involves the following procedure:

JANUARY -	New Year's card sent to the customer;
FEBRUARY -	Newsletter sent
MARCH -	Networking function after hours
APRIL -	Newsletter sent
MAY -	Telephone call - to gain customer data
JUNE -	Newsletter sent
JULY -	End of financial year drinks function
AUGUST -	Newsletter sent
SEPTEMBER -	"How's things going?" Follow-up phone call
OCTOBER -	Newsletter sent
NOVEMBER -	Special article written about their industry
DECEMBER -	Christmas fax

Follow-up contact program for prospects who don't purchase

This is the procedure we use for these prospects:

After the Information Kit is sent:

WEEK 2.	Last copy of our newsletter sent
WEEK 4.	Follow-up telephone call
WEEK 6.	Vision summary referral
WEEK 8.	McGirvan Media audio tape sent
WEEK 10.	They become part of our regular contact program

Flow Chart of A Service Selling System - In Store Selling

- **Prior to the prospective customer visiting your store**
  Make sure the store is clean, tidy and everyone is in uniform with his or her name tags. All point-of-sale material is well displayed and up-to-date.

- **Customer greeting**
  The customer is greeted and the customer service person introduces themselves.The customer is greeted upon entering the store. It may be by a simple "Good Morning/Good Afternoon, how can I help you?" or you may want to be different and want to say, "I know that you are looking. My name is ...., if I can be of any assistance I will be over there." If it is busy in the store the customer is greeted and acknowledged if they are going to be kept waiting by saying "Good Morning, I won't be a moment.Thank you for waiting." This is an opportunity to ask some open questions such as, "What in particular may you be looking for?" Check if they have made a purchase from your store before.

- **Questioning process to understand the customer's needs**
  It is appropriate to ask a couple of open questions to understand how you can best meet the customer's needs. Find out what the customer wants to achieve. If they have a budget in mind, identify a buying motivator and ask if they have used this product before.

  The question process is done in a relaxed and casual way. Here are some sample questions you may want to ask the customer:

  - What do you want this product to do for you specifically?
  - How much have you thought about investing?
  - What's most important when you buy a product like this one?
  - What type of experience have you had with this product in the past?

- **Providing a solution to the customer**
  Once you know the customer's needs and buying motivators, then make sure you describe how you feel that particular product will best meet their needs.Tell them about the benefits of that product. Don't talk just about the features of the product and ensure you relate the benefits to their specific needs.

- Cross-selling opportunity

  During the time that you are talking with your customer you need to be actively listening for additional opportunities to recommend some of your other products. The joining phase may be as simple as:
  - "You mentioned that you were interested in ... Is that important to you?"
  - "Can I suggest that you look at ....?"
  - "Are you also aware that we provide ....?"
  - "Could I recommend this new ....?"
  - "Is there anything else I can assist you with today?"

- Completing the transaction

  Ask closing questions to complete the transaction if needed. Complete the warranty card for the customer. Count out the change into the customer's hand if it is a cash sale. Ask them if they want the product wrapped. Have the customer complete a customer information card for your store V.I.P. Program and explain the benefits of that program to them. Check if they have any additional questions for you. Let them know you will give them a follow-up call in a week's time.

- Thank you and farewell

  Give them two of your store cards, write your name on them for future reference and ask them to give these to friends as a referral. Offer to carry the product to their car. Look them in the eye and say "Thank you" as you walk them to the store door, or to their car.

- Customer administration

  Place all the customer's details on the computer system and give them an initial customer classification level. If they are an existing customer, enter the purchase into your computer system.

- Thank-you note

  This is written the day of the transaction and sent the next day.

- **Follow-up phone call**

  Contact the customer four to five days after the product purchase. Ask if they have any questions and, once again, thank them for their purchase.

- **Database loyalty program**

  This customer is classified and put into a loyalty program which could include the following procedure:

JANUARY	New Year's card sent to the customer;
APRIL	Newsletter sent
JULY	New financial year sale for V.I.P. customers with your newsletter
OCTOBER	Newsletter and invitation for V.I.P. after hours function
DECEMBER	Christmas greeting note

Now, take some time to look at every step of your service selling experience and identify ways to improve it. It could be a specific process or a software application introduced or making better use of current technology available in your marketplace. I heard a guy called Wayne Cotton speak once and he had a great saying "If it is a problem, make it a process and you won't have a problem any more". Use processes to solve your problems and you will build a consistent business.

The seven points of contact philosophy

This concept is about building the trust and credibility with the customer during your service selling experience. The philosophy predicts that it takes seven positive points of contact with your customers before they trust you enough to make a big-ticket purchase. In other words, you need to make seven deposits into their rapport building bank account before they will make any deposits into your financial bank account. The points of contact could be as simple as a phone call, sending out your brochure when you said you would or making a follow-up call to answer any questions. It could be a positive face-to-face meeting or providing a quote to do the work. We use this in our business and it has made a huge difference to our sales conversion rates, by simply making sure that we have made seven points of contact before we ask the customer to buy our product. It is a great technique to use if you have a long sales process.

The 6 loyalty implementation steps

Here are the 6 steps you need to have in place if your loyalty system is going to work in your business.

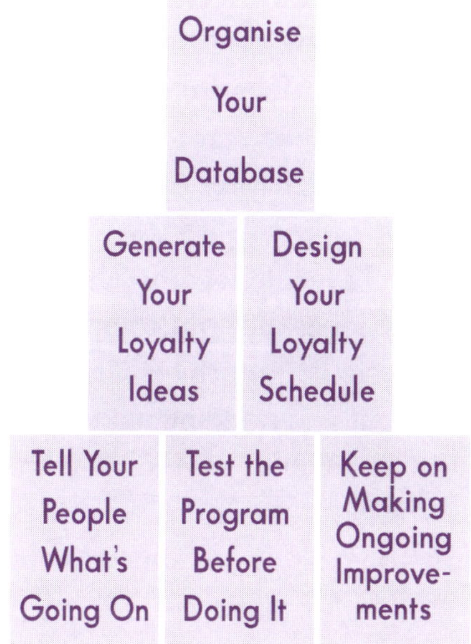

1. Organise Your Database

Get your database up and running. It needs to be a computer database that is user friendly. If you have one already in place, organise it so that you can record your customer details and be able to generate direct contact either by telephone, fax, letter or e-mail. Make sure that you have your database classified and it has been up-dated. If you don't have a database in place, now's the time to put one in. In the next chapter, I will give you the key strategies to set up an operational database to use when developing your customer loyalty program.

2. Generate your loyalty ideas

I am always on the lookout for a great way to generate greater customer loyalty from my database. Keep your eyes and ears open for different ways to stay in touch with your customers, to continue to give them a reason to return to your business: look in the paper: talk to other industries. In chapter 6, I have put together 47 ways on how you can gain greater customer loyalty from your customers. These are tried and proven methods with easy-to-implement instructions for you to follow. At this point in time you are looking at anywhere from twelve ideas, i.e. one per month for your "A" customers to perhaps four per year for your "C" customers. I know you will find these ideas in chapter 6 both beneficial and practical.

3. Designing your 12 month loyalty schedule

Now take your loyalty ideas and put them into an action plan for the next twelve months. 12 months is a good timeframe because the time slips by without you noticing it and all of a sudden another month rolls by and you haven't started, or worse still you start but then you got busy being busy and drop the ball. Here are some suggestions on how to go about organising your schedule. Do it by customer classifications, for example:

- Your "A" customers you may plan to contact every month,
- Your "B" customers every 60 days,
- Your "C" customers every 90 days.

Get yourself a calendar and map out your loyalty activities on it. Then put together an advanced plan of action when things need to done by. An example of this is, if my newsletter is due to be sent in July, then I will write it in May for printing in June and posting in July. Plan ahead or it will never happen. Here is just a sample of what your 6-month loyalty schedule may look like.

Customer Loyalty Schedule

Month	*"A" Customers*	*"B" Customers*	*"C" Customers*
January	New Year's Card	New Year's Card	No Activity
February	Personal Call	Special Offer	No Activity
March	Newsletter	Newsletter	Newsletter
April	Personal Note	No Activity	No Activity
May	Invitation	Personal Call	No Activity
June	Newsletter	Newsletter	Newsletter

4. Get your people involved in the process

If your people are going to take ownership of creating customer loyalty, then they need to be involved in creating the ideas and the schedule to make this system work in your business. Get your people involved in the process and keep everyone informed as to what you are doing to develop customer loyalty. This is important when your people are talking to customers. If the customer mentions a special offer they received from you last week and your staff member does not know anything about it, then what will the customer think of your business? Get your people involved in the process and they could come up with some of your best loyalty gaining ideas.

5. Test everything you do

Before you go out and launch a new offer or organise this huge customer function, take time to go and test your ideas with some of your customers. Contact a cross section of five or ten or twenty customers and tell them what you are thinking about doing and ask them if they would be interested in participating. Gain their feedback and see if your idea is worth pursuing. You might have the best idea in the world; but the problem is that you are looking at it from your world, not your customers.

6. Continuous ongoing improvements

Ideas that worked this year may not work next year. You need to always be looking out for ways to build the customer relationship and enhance your customer loyalty. Whatever you do, look to improve it and you will never become obsolete in your marketplace.

Chapter 4 - Practical business projects

The following questions will assist you in clarifying what you need to change or improve in your service selling system to give your customers a memorable experience.

1. What do you do well when it comes to service selling?

____

____

____

____

2. What do you need to improve upon when it comes to service selling in your business?

____

____

____

____

3. What are some of the strategies you need to implement to improve your service selling in your business?

____

____

____

____

4. What other roadblocks stop your people from giving a memorable service selling experience to your customers?

____

____

____

____

Chapter 5 – Positioning

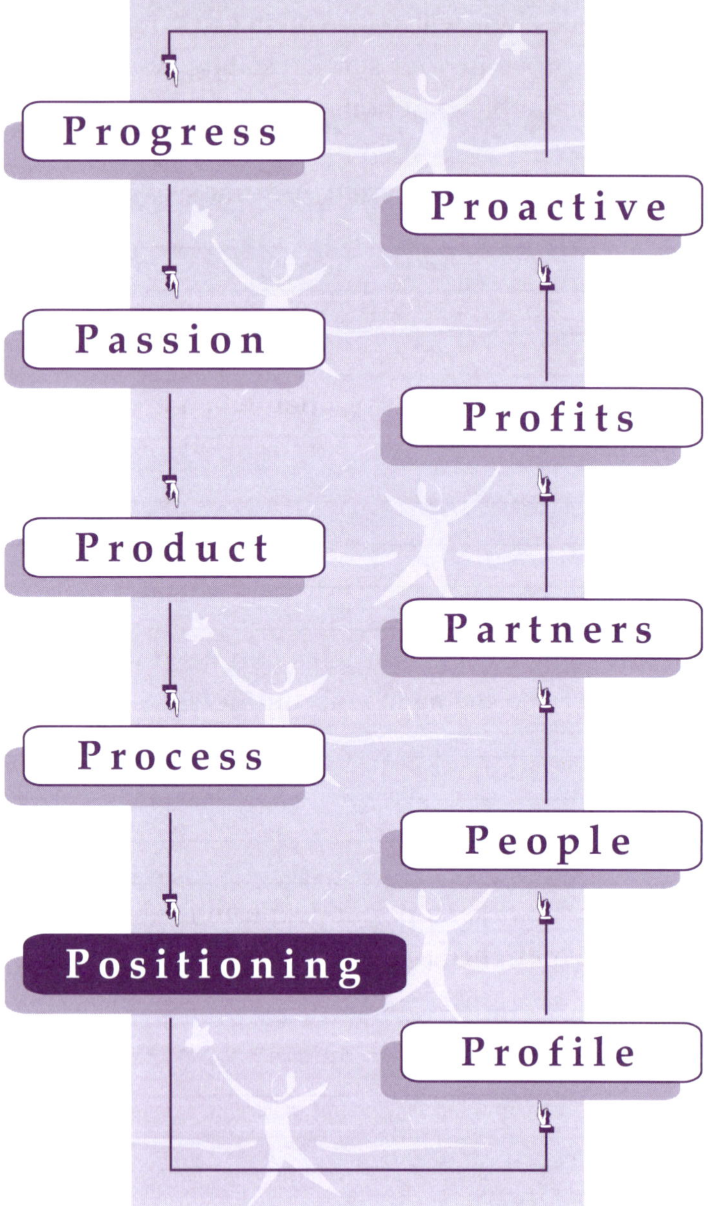

Creating Loyal Profitable Customers

Creating a unique point-of-difference that sets you apart

"If your customer cannot differentiate between you and your competitor, they will make a choice based on price and not on value."

In today's marketplace our customers have so many choices on where to get their products or services from that is it no wonder that people get confused. One of your goals in business should be to create a point-of-difference that makes you memorable, unique and drives a wedge between your business and that of your competitors so that the choice is an easy one for your customers.

Own the mountain in your marketplace

What happens is we go into business with the belief that our product is better than our competitors for a number of reasons. But if the truth is known, from our customer's point of view, there is no point-of-difference.The reason for that is we have positioned ourselves on the same mountain in our marketplace as our competitors.

This is the same mountain we are all trying to climb so eventually we arrive at the summit.The challenge is creating a new mountain for our businesses to own. I believe there are two mountains to choose from: 'the mass-market mountain' or 'the niche-market mountain'. On the mass-market mountain you compete with everyone and it is getting more and more difficult to create a point of real difference to set you apart.

On the niche-market mountain you can make it your own. You can create it, dominate it and make it very difficult for your competitors to climb it.

The diagrams below give you a visual insight into the concept of "Owning the mountain in your marketplace".

Competing on the Mass Market Mountain model

Many people have beaten the same path up the same mountain.

Competing on the mass market mountain in the marketplace

- Many competitors to be compared with always
- Hard to create a real point-of-difference
- Customers focus on just the product
- The market is very price sensitive
- Hard to dominate for a long period of time

Determine the mountain you want to own and dominate, as both will require a different strategy for your business to pursue.

Owning the Mountain in Your Marketplace Model

Owning your own mountain in your marketplace

- Fewer competiors to be compared with
- Easy to create a point-of-difference
- You can focus on your area of expertise
- Your market is not as price sensitive
- Easy to dominate to build your brand loyalty

Discover your own mountain in your own market place and you will find, very few people have ever tried to climb it.

Now, if your products are the same as your competitors you may wish to create a point-of-difference by targeting a specific niche market that is made up of a demographic group that you relate best to or who have a need that is not currently being catered for. It may be looking at a specific type of price shopper in your marketplace, one at the top end of the market who doesn't mind paying extra for a superior level of service that they receive from you, or it could be the price-conscious shopper who is just looking for a deal.The key now is to identify the type of mountain you want to own in your marketplace.

Look at some of the products in our international marketplace that have created a point-of-difference. Volvo has created a point of difference around its safety features, Bang & Olufsen Hi-Fi equipment has created a unique point-of-difference with their compact, sleek looking quality hi-fi equipment catering for the music listening enthusiast.

When you think of fine writing instruments the company Waterman Pens comes to mind.Their pens do the same job as any other pen but the company has created a point-of-difference by their design, style, reputation and reliability.All of these companies have created their own unique point-of-difference or, in other words, they own their specific mountain in their marketplace.

In the following section you will find some questions to assist you in identifying your Mountain in your Marketplace.

Sending the right messages into your marketplace

Everything you do sends a message into your marketplace and to your customers. How does your marketplace perceive you and your product? What are you famous for in your customer's eyes? Here are some questions to get you thinking about the unique position you are looking to create.

- What messages are you sending into your marketplace?
- What is your point-of-difference that sets you apart?
- What are you famous for in your marketplace?
- What is the perfect niche market for your business?
- Whom do you love to deal with in your business?
- How would your customers best describe you, your people, your product and your service?

Identify your customer niche

One of the best ways to identify your niche is to paint a picture of the perfect customer for your business. What customers do you love to deal with? What customers are the most profitable and professional to work for or with? An easy way to do this is to look at your top 20% of customers as I have mentioned previously in this book, and identify what they all have in common; it could be a common need or amount of money they spend with you each month; or where they live; or how they came to use your products and services in the first place.

Once you have done this, then you can start to develop a strategy to get more customers like these. It will make a big difference in how you market to these people.

History is 20/20 vision and a great information source for your future, only if you use it to your advantage.

Every mistake is a learning opportunity, only if you learn from it.

The buying influences that impacts on your customers

Your customers are influenced by a number of different buying triggers. These triggers can be used to determine how you identify your top 20% of customers. Here are some of the reasons why your customers may buy your product.

- People buy the product because it costs less.
- People buy the product because it is easy to use or obtain.
- People buy the product because someone has referred them to that product.
- People buy the product because it is a recognised brand name.
- People buy the product because of the additional value they get from it.
- People buy the product because it will solve a challenge or meet a specific need.
- People buy the product because they trust and respect the person selling it to them.
- People buy the product because of results they have received previously.
- People buy the product because they get more for their money.
- People buy the product because it is a low risk purchase.

People buy for their reasons, not for your reasons. Your goal in business is to find out those reasons and make your product appealing to those reasons. Once you understand your customer base and start to target like-minded customers you will see some buying trends appear in your customer base. Monitor these trends and design special product offers and your marketing campaign around them.

Working smarter by classifying your customer base

I have been a great believer in classifying your customer database, so that you know where to spend your time most effectively. Do you spend most of your time with your "A" customers or your "D" customers? In working smarter I think you need to review the following keys when you classify your database.

- Have you got your customer's details on a computer database or customer contact management system?
- Have you designed a customer classification system on your database?
- Have you classified all of your current customers and prospects?
- Have you defined the different service levels or standards for each customer classification?
- Have you identified the strategies to take your "B" customers to "A" customers

Let's look at each one of these areas and discuss some of the ways to use them in your business with your customers:

Setting Up Your Customer Database

What I would recommend is that you go into your marketplace and research the best computer database or customer contact system. There are a number of very good software programs on the market from ACT, Maximizer, Goldmine and Sales Logix.There could even be some programs that have been specifically written for your industry.The key things you are looking for in a customer contact software program are the following:-

- You can generate a letter, fax or e-mail from the software program to the customer.
- You can record all their details from name, address, and contact numbers, personal details or make any special notes.
- You can look up any particular group of people on your database. They could include everyone in a certain area, all of your "B" customers or customers that have not purchased from you in the last six months.

- You want to be able to merge a group of your customers into a word processing template.

You also want to be able to customise your computer screen template to your business needs. With quality databases as I have previously mentioned, you will have a variety of template choices that may suit your business. If not, they will have a command where you can change this template to suit your specific needs.

The next step is to identify the key areas you want to record on your computer database, areas such as;-

Name	Address	Telephone
Fax #	E-mail Address	Website
Where you met them	Their title or position	Company Name

You may want to think about some of the other areas that you want to record or include when setting up your database, such as: -

Date of birth	Past products purchased	Family names
Special offers sent out	Company History	Hobbies
Special interests	Staff members' names	Sports played
Mobile phone number	Classification listing	Referrals given
Invitations sent	Their preferences	Any special notes

As I mentioned previously, make sure you can produce letters, faxes and e-mails from your database as this is one feature that is a must when developing customer loyalty.

Designing your customer classification system

As time is becoming one of our most valued assets in the information age we live in, you and I need to make sure we spend each hour wisely. One of the best ways to do this is to make sure we are spending the time with the right customers. Here are some easy-to-follow steps you should take in order to classify your customer database. This will not only maximise your potential, but also your profits.

1. Decide on your classification system

There are a number of different ways to classify your customers. You could use a colour coding system - Red; Blue; Black & White. It could be by metals - Bronze; Silver; Gold; Platinum. The system I prefer is simply - "A, B, C, D". The other classifications I use are for prospects, and our general database. You need to work out the system that best suits your business.

2. Identify your top 20% of customers

You should look at your top 20% of customers. I think we are familiar with the 80/20 rule, i.e. 80% of your income will come from 20% of your customers. To see if this is true for your business, look at your top 20% of customers and work out how much income they give you. If you have not done this before it is a great exercise to do for your business.

- Who are your top 20%?
- What do they look like?
- What types of products do they buy?
- How often do they buy from you?
- What types of businesses are they in? What is their demographic make-up?

3. How will you rank your customer base?

Here are some ways to classify your customers. Think about these areas to determine how you will best rank your customers: -

- How many purchases do they make in a set time frame?
- How much money do they spend with you in a specific time frame - Week; Month; Year?

- How many of your products do they use?
- Are they professional to deal with?
- Do they pay on time?
- How profitable is each of their transactions for your business?
- How many referrals do they give to your business?

One of my customers has used not one, but three specific criteria to classify their customer base. For them it is done by current income, future income potential and how progressive that customers' business is. They have used these three criteria to assess each customer so they get a total picture and not just a one-sided snapshot.

I read an interesting article from the Harvard Business Review, in the July/August, 1996 edition, titled *Strategic Renewal for Business Units* written by John O. Whitney. He talked about a great system and approach to client loyalty including relating the three dimensions when measuring your customers. This was called S.S.P. which stands for S - Strategic Importance, S - Significance and P- Profitability. The author asks you to look at it from these three dimensions. It's a great article and one worth reading.

Classify all of your current customers

Decide how you will classify your customer base, and then do it. It will take time but you will find business opportunities you never thought you had. Make sure you review your customer classification regularly to make any changes and to keep pace with the buying habits of your customers. Identify at the same time the potential for growth each one of these customers will have in your business.

Different service levels and frequency of contact for each customer classification level

This is one area people sometimes have a challenge understanding. The bottom line is you give everyone great service. But for your "A" customers, you give absolutely unbelievably fantastic service. Why? Because they spend more money, or buy more products or refer you onto more people than a "D" customer does, and "A" customers are harder to replace if you lose them to a competitor. Your very best customers need better turnaround times, a quick service lane or greater frequency of interaction from you with your customer loyalty program. By having a varying level of service it sends a clear and concise message to your people as to who to treat as a VIP and a clear message to your customers that you look after those customers who are loyal to your business.

Identify the strategies to take your "B" customers to "A" customers

Once you have identified where your customers are situated on your database, then you can start to plan how you are going to take them to the next level.Take a close look at your customer database and identify the "C" customers who could be your "A" customers. Why are they not "A" customers? It could be that they don't fully appreciate everything you do and so they only buy one product from you, instead of three or four. Perhaps you have not given them enough reasons to make a second or third purchase from you.

Design some specific strategies or a marketing plan to take your "C" customers to "B" customers and "B" customers to "A" customers. By understanding this concept you can not only save time and money, but concentrate your energies on areas that will give you your greatest return.

Build your business, from referrals. It's a great point-of-difference

Ever since I started my own business I have built it on referrals. We had an unlisted office telephone number and an unlisted personal telephone number. So if we didn't work off referrals we would have been out of business a long time ago. This approach has given us a unique point-of-difference. As you can imagine I'm a great believer in working off referrals. Once again, it is another way to create a point-of-difference in your marketplace, not to mention that it is the most powerful form of marketing there is available and, most importantly it is cost effective.

In this part of the chapter I would like to give you a number of different strategies you can use to gain referrals from your customers, whether it be through an in-store selling situation or if you are a salesperson working in a direct selling situation.

9 steps to gain more referrals in a direct selling situation

1. *Plant the seed with your customer*

Let your customer, or prospective customer know that you work off referrals in your business. If they are totally happy and satisfied with the product and service you provide, then ask them if they would consider referring you on to like- minded people or associates. What you are endeavouring to do is to create an expectation up front that you work off referrals.

2. *Tell referral stories at meetings*

Share stories of other customers that have been referred to you for your services. Water the seed you planted at the first meeting. It may be as simple as relating a situation about your customers that have been referred to you. Once again, we are just trying to paint the picture that you prefer working off referrals.

3. Check if the customer is 100% totally happy and satisfied with you

After you have completed the job, or provided the product to your customer, check if the customer is totally happy and satisfied with your product or service before asking for any referrals. Remember, unsatisfied customers don't give referrals.

4. Asking for referrals from your customers

Before you ask for referrals think about your approach with your customer. The phrase I use is simply "Whom do you know that could benefit from the products and services I provide?" At this point in time you may want to share with the customer the profile of the perfect prospect for your business. You may also want to prompt your customer about the different types of people you currently work with.

5. The four ways to contact the referrals

There are four ways to contact the referrals that you have been given. You can call them and use the customer's name as a point of reference or the customer can call the referral. Then you call them. Another way is your customer can write to them with your details or brochure and then you will call the referral. Finally, one of the best ways, but also the most difficult to set up, is where your customer sets a three way meeting between you, your customer and their associate whom they want to refer to you.

6. Think about your approach to the person who has been referred to you

I believe you should write out your approach and script it. However, I don't believe you should read off the script, word for word. Prepare yourself mentally so you can produce the best possible effect.

7. Contact the prospective new customer

All referrals have a shelf life, so don't take forever to contact them. Here is a sample of a script approach that we have used with sales people from a number of different industries.

Script for approaching a prospect who has been referred to you

1. Hi ...., My name is (Your name from your business name) - You don't know me! But your name has been given to me by .... He/She asked me to give you a call because he/she thought you may be able to benefit from the services our business have been providing to his/her company.

2. (Prospect's name), have you got a moment to talk now?

3. If the response is "No" - That's O.K. - When's a good time to call back or can I send you some information? What is your address?

4. If the response is "Yes" - Great! We have been helping (Referrer's Name) with XYZ services/products.

5. Can I ask you - from time to time, does your business need services/products like these? (Explain the real benefits of your products/services)?

6. If the response is "No" - That's O.K. Is there anyone else whom you know that could benefit from our services/products? Who would be the best person to talk to in your business? Where are they located? Do you have a contact number? Yes - Great. What I'd like to do is send you some information about our products and services.

7. (Prospect's Name), what I will do now is put this information in the mail to you, then I will give you a follow up call to make sure you received it and to see if there is an opportunity for us to get together at some stage. Is that O.K.?

8. (Prospect's Name), what's the best address to send this information to?

   [Check Spelling of Name & Address]

9. Thank you for your time today (Prospect's Name). I look forward to speaking with you in a week's time. Bye. [Hang Up Last]

8. Feedback to your customer

It is important for the continuation of the referral process that you complete the loop and get back in touch with your customer and let them know what happened with the person they referred to you. Once again thank them for helping you build your business and their support. Who knows they may even have another referral for you.

9. Reward your customers who gives referrals

Always remember what gets rewarded, gets repeated. If you want to get your customer to give you additional referrals, write them a note to say thank you or send them a small gift. Whether anything happens as a result of that referral or not, reward them.

In-Store selling situation

Some of the referral gaining principles here are the same as those in the direct selling situation. However, here are some other strategies you can use in your business:

- Give the customer two of your business cards. One card for them and one for a friend. If their friend brings your card into the store, they will receive a special gift when they purchase something or they will go into the prize draw even if they don't purchase something from your store or business.

- Plant the seed with your customers. Let your customers know that people are being referred to you on a regular basis. So if they are totally happy and satisfied they will be happy to refer you to friends, family and associates. Create the right expectation with your customers. This could be done through your newsletter, store or notice board.

- Organise a "bring a friend night" for your customers. Let them know you are having a special night after hours in the store just for VIP customers and let them know they are welcome to bring a friend or associate on the night. You may have an interesting speaker with a popular topic. It's important that you capture the friend's name for future follow-up. A great way to do this is to have a lucky door prize with everyone's business card.

- Ask your customers for referrals. "Whom do you know that could benefit from our products and services we offer?" If they enjoy your service and products you won't be able to stop them telling their friends.

- Print on the back of your business card, "The greatest compliment we can receive is when our customers refer us onto their friends. Please give this card to a friend or associate for a discount the next time they visit our store."

- Get out into your marketplace and promote your business and services. Take the opportunity to go and speak to some local groups like the Chamber of Commerce, Rotary Clubs, Apex or networking organisations in your local community. Create a profile for yourself so that people know what you do, how you do it and how people can benefit from using your services and products.

- Welcome new customers who have been referred to you, either in your business newsletter or on a special board located in your store or business. Make a big deal about it. Remember it is your responsibility to educate your customers.

You create your own positioning. However too many times we go into our marketplace with a shotgun approach, instead of thinking about whom we want to do business with. Positioning is about working smarter to build your business, to maximise your marketplace potential.

Chapter 5 - Practical business projects

Please answer the following questions to assist you in clarifying what your position is currently and where it should be in the future.

1. What are you and your business famous for?

2. Who makes up your top 20% of your customers? What do they look like?

3. How are you going to classify your customer base, or if you already have your customer base classified, do you need to review it?

4. What strategies are you going to use to take your "C" customers to "B" customers and your "B" customers to "A" customers?

Chapter 6 – Profile

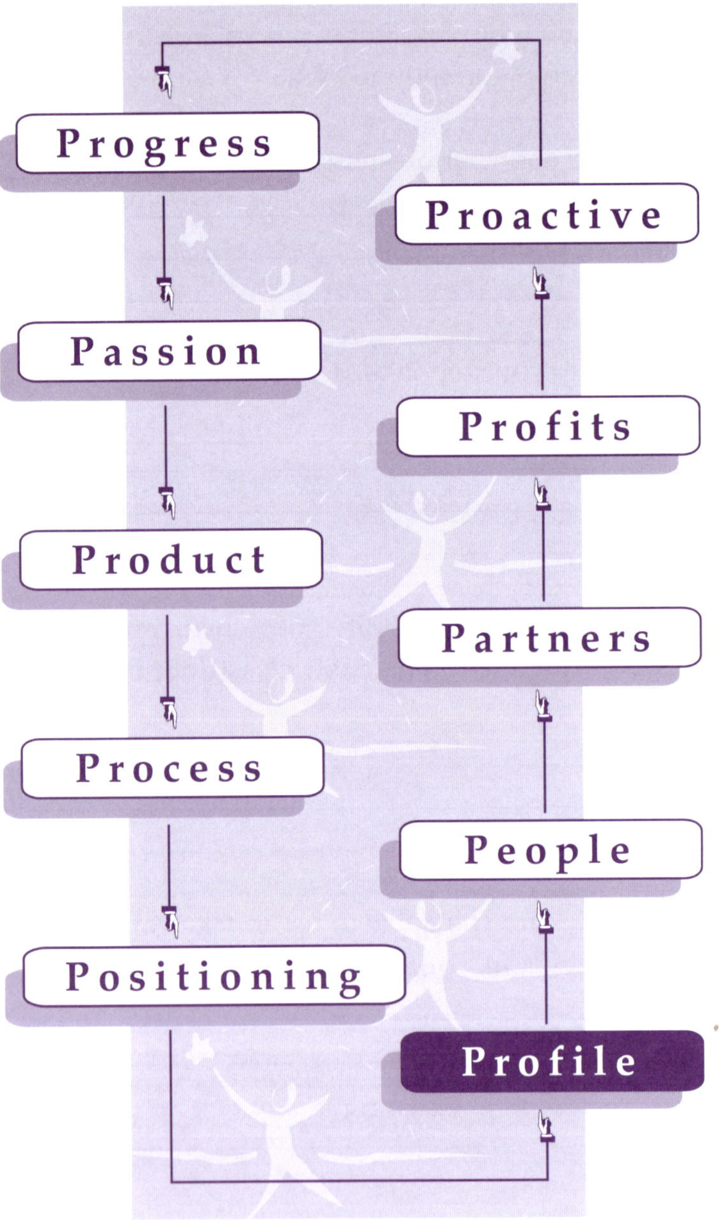

Creating Loyal Profitable Customers

PROFILE

Creating a customer loyalty system that works in your business - 47 ways to gain greater customer loyalty

"Client loyalty is doing the extraordinary to distinguish you from the ordinary in the marketplace."

The goal when creating customer loyalty is about giving your customers an unexpected positive experience that keeps you and your product at the top of their mind. Your goal is to have a frequent interaction with the customer. When the time arrives for them to purchase your product again, they think about you and your business first.

The key is to stay in touch with your customer when they don't need your product or services and by doing this you start to add value. This value is often the point-of-difference that sets you apart and stops your competitors moving in on your key customers.

Remember, it is always easier for your competitors to steal your market share rather than trying to find a new customer who has never purchased that type of product before. By using some of the following loyalty gaining ideas you not only give your customers a reason to return to your business, but you also build a brick wall around your customers against the influence of your competitors.

The following ideas have been gained from around the world and tested to work in our marketplace. Yet the amount of people who use these techniques to master their marketplace is limited which is good news for you and me as it makes it easy to create that unique point-of-difference.

1. Personalised thank-you notes

I think one of the most powerful ways to create a point of difference is by saying "Thank you for your business" or "I appreciate the opportunity to meet with you". Less than 2% ever say thank you in writing. Think about your last five major purchases, did you ever get a note to say thank you for making that purchase?

The important issue here is, when you write the note, make sure it is hand written. Think about it, when was the last time you received a hand written note, saying thank you in the last 6 months? It will set you apart and your customers will rave about you.

2. What to do if you don't get the product sale

Just as you say thank you for the business, you need to say thank you even if you don't get the sale, contract, win the quote or if you are not the successful applicants. Before you say "Why do I need to do that?" you will see that there are basically two reasons. Firstly, because you were given an opportunity to be considered in the first place. Some people are not even asked.

Secondly, you get the last say and, if the successful business drops the ball or does not produce the right results, then you are at the top of the list for next time. You may even get re-considered because you went the extra mile.

How many people are totally 100% satisfied after they make their purchasing decision? Remember, 60% of people give up after the first "no" and 95% of sales people have given up after the sixth "no". Perseverance is a positive, proactive approach.

3. Follow-up phone calls

Everything you do needs to be followed up with a note, phone call, personal visit or e-mail. Never assume that your prospective customer received the information in the post; is totally happy with the purchase; is able to work out how to use the product; or has had all questions answered. So few people follow up a product sale or request for information.

Recently I purchased a new computer and data projection unit for the keynote presentations I do at conferences. I contacted five companies to supply the equipment. All five companies sent me their information and prices but only one of them gave me a follow-up call to see if I received the information, if I had any questions and if I would like a free demonstration.

Which company do you think I placed my $20,000 order with? What I think is funny is that the other four companies are probably sitting around their boardroom tables at a Monday morning sales meeting and talking about how tough the market is at the moment and how no one is making any purchasing decisions. Give me a break!

4. Prior notice of new products or your sale

If you are about to launch a new product or update some of your product range let your customers know in advance. Don't let them find out through the media or by someone else. It is a perfect way to continue to educate your customers about the benefits of your products. This could be done by a letter, fax or e-mail. You may want to give them an inviting offer to purchase or try your new product.

I do most of my shopping at what I believe is one of Australia's finest menswear stores, Mitchell Ogilvie Menswear in Brisbane City. One of the things that keeps me coming back is that he lets me know, as a regular customer, two weeks in advance of his sale date so that I can purchase my product at sale prices without the hassle of going to his twice-yearly sale. Mitch gives me a reason to return and makes me feel special about it all at the same time.

5. Product-of-the-month focus

By the way, if you don't have new products you may want to have a product-of-the-month focus. Even if your customers don't buy your product, you are once again taking the opportunity to educate your customers about what you do and sell. Give them a special to entice them to try it, check it out when they are next in your store or perhaps give them a free demonstration in their home or business.

6. Personal birthday greetings

You may want to write a note, send a birthday card or even an electronic greeting card via e-mail to your customers. During my seminars people often question the sincerity of these cards and the point I make is that, if you have done nothing to build the relationship or stay in contact during the year, then this activity is about as sincere as polyester. It may come across as very fake. However, if you are adding value to them or their business at other times during the year, then it is quite acceptable and appreciated.

How do you capture your customer's date of birth? You can simply ask them, keep your ears open for those little hints, or ask their people when their manager's birthday is. (But only ask them for the day and month - not the year!!) You may also have them fill out a survey. This process is also worthwhile completing with some of their key people whom you deal with on a regular basis. Remember, these people are often part of the decision-making process.

7. Company anniversary

Take a moment to send a card or fax to the company and employees on the anniversary of its foundation. You may even want to congratulate them with a gift or send them a birthday cake. This information can usually be found by checking their company brochure, visiting their website or by asking their people within the company. Few people do this, but if you conducted this loyalty gaining activity, what would your customers think about you?

8. Product purchase anniversary

Contact your customers at times relating to the history of the product. It could be that you contact them about 12 months after the purchase to give them an update on your business or simply to check that everything is going well with that product. You may want to let people know that the product is just about to come off warranty and offer to check it for them. At this point it may be an opportunity to offer some type of special up selling offer for an extended warranty or maintenance agreement.

9. Your company's birthday celebrations

Many companies tell you about their birthday sale or celebrations. But perhaps a nice touch would be if you thanked your customers for helping you continue being in business. Without their business you wouldn't be having too many more birthdays! You could send a sincere note, or even an advertisement attached to some type of editorial about your business in the local paper or your association publication.

10. Deliver your information with an unexpected gift

Give people the unexpected and they will be pleasantly surprised. Recently we sent our new information kit to a number of key prospects. To have the desired impact and to ensure that we created a point of difference, we attached helium balloons to the package. When the balloons were delivered the interest we created in the prospect's office was amazing. What was even more amazing was the feedback we got when we gave them a follow-up call. "So you are the people who sent the balloons, yes I know that Ms. ..., wants to talk to you", were some of the comments. All 30 prospects we called took our follow-up call or returned our call.

That exercise cost us under $200 and to date we have booked over $25,000 of work from that one exercise. You may not use balloons but come up with an idea that suits your business. I like what Kwik Kopy Printing do when they send your printing order; they place a box of lollies in the top of the box of printing.

11. "How do we improve?" customer meetings

I have been a strong advocate of obtaining feedback from some of your key customers. You see, you and I get too close to our own businesses. By asking your customer to give you this type of feedback you receive a different perspective of your business through your customer's eyes. In our own business we run two customer meetings each year and the feedback is invaluable to our future planning process.

At this meeting our customers give us our best ideas and a clear understanding of what else we can do to add value to their business in the coming year. They also give us feedback on what we need to improve in our business. We take this information away, develop new products, improve our service processes and we sell these services back to our customers. The funny thing about it is that they purchase them! Why? Because they are their ideas, not ours.

Here is an agenda on how to conduct this meeting. For a hard copy of this meeting agenda, visit my website at http://www.ppp.net.au and you will be able to download it for your purposes.

CUSTOMER FEEDBACK MEETING AGENDA

Set the Scene

- Thank you for your time
- Explain the reason for the meeting - Gain feedback, ideas and suggestions for improvements
- Explain the approach you are going to take during the meeting - by asking questions
- Explain the benefit to your business and to them the customer
- Give people an overview of your business, what you have achieved and your future goals

Questions to ask

1. From your point of view what do we do well as a business?

2. What would you like us to improve or where do you think we could improve?

3. If we wanted to become famous for our service or products, what would we need to do differently in order to achieve that?

4. What else could we do to create an exceptional customer service experience in our business?

5. What could we do to add greater value to the service transaction between yourself and our business?

6. What else could we do to build a stronger relationship with you and our other customers?

7. What is the biggest problem you face when dealing with people in my line of work, industry or business? What are things that stop you from doing business with them?

8. From your point of view, what do these people need to do to fix these problems?

Wrap Up

- Thank them for their time, ideas and feedback.
- Give a small gift perhaps.

Points to Think About

- Use a tape recorder to record the meeting so that you don't miss anything.
- Stick to a timetable.
- Jot everyone a note after the meeting to say thank you.
- Make sure you introduce everyone around, so that people are comfortable when it comes to putting their ideas forward.
- Never defend or try to justify why you have done something. Remember everyone's opinion is right in his or her own mind.

12. Networking function

As I have mentioned before, your most valuable asset in the future will be your database. Think about your customers, how many of your customers could do business with some of your other customers. Your role could be to introduce some of your key customers to each other. You may run this function as an informal after-hours event with a select group of people. Plan this function professionally and think about which customers would appreciate meeting other customers in your database. Your role at this function is to ensure that everyone feels welcome and gets a chance to meet, mix and mingle.

13. Put into place a referral system

Ask your customers for referrals. Happy customers are happy to refer you onto like-minded people. But you need to ask for those referrals. It could be as simple as the ways I mentioned in Chapter 4. Remember people who have referred their friends to your business are in the process of becoming loyal advocates of you and your business. It could be as simple as giving your advocates two business cards, one for them and one for a friend. On the back of the cards make sure you write your customer's name so you know who to thank when the prospective customer walks in with your card.

14. Make available your library of information

If you have a number of books, tapes, articles or industry related material in your business why not put some of this information together in a catalogue and make them available to your customers. It could be an additional service you promote to your customers, or it could be a faxed out special offer as a free service. Before you get concerned that you may become a librarian overnight, on average 95% of your customers will never use this service. But what will they think about you because you offered it to them?

15. Special program for your "A" customers

You need to look after your "A" customers, as they are hard to replace. Don't take them for granted.These customers may need a shorter contact cycle, at least every 30 days, if not shorter, depending on your business and product. Make sure everyone in your business knows whom these people are so that they know to go the extra mile for them when necessary.

16. Movie night

One of my clients conducted a movie night where he hired out a movie theatre and arranged for a pre-release movie to be shown. He only invited 50 "A" Customers and asked each one to bring a like-minded associate. These "A" Customers will refer you to prospective "A" Customers. It was a great customer loyalty function. It was also a great networking event, but most of all, it was a great way to gain 50 new referrals.

17. Business newsletter

I don't know if you have ever thought about writing either your own newsletter or for your customer's newsletters.There are some basic rules when writing your newsletter.The first is that you need to use the 80/20 Rule. Eighty percent of your newsletter needs to be; how people can save time or money; make more money; make people more productive or how people can improve their lifestyle. The 20% needs to be about you, your business and your products. If you mix up this formula, people will not read your newsletter.

Listed below are a few other points you could include in your newsletter to make it compulsory reading by your customers.

- Use satisfied customer testimonials
- Profile one of your staff members - their background, role & experience
- Interview some of your more interesting or famous customers
- Use an interesting headline for your newsletter articles
- Give some hints and tips about points of interest - sport, travel, entertainment
- Profile one of your new or popular products
- Welcome any new customers by name
- Thank those customers who have referred customers to you
- Recommend other strategically aligned services that would be of value
- Include a photo of yourself or your business to create some visual association
- Use quotes, examples or human interest stories in your newsletter

Your goal, when you write your newsletter, is to have people contact you and have your customers feel that you are adding value to them and their business. If you would like to see an example of our newsletter then visit our website: http://www.ppp.net.au. If you want to receive our quarterly newsletter "The Passion Report", you can fax or send us an e-mail.

18. Find unique ways to thank your customers

Be different when you go to thank your customers. Find unique and different ways to say "Thank you" or "We appreciate your business". One of the things we have done that got a great response is we gave a bottle of wine as a thank-you gift. We teamed up with a winemaker and got him to autograph the bottle of wine for our customer. This was very well received. Other gifts we have given have been: framed motivational postcards; movie tickets; gift voucher for a specialty retail shop; day spa massage; car wash and a dinner for two. Here is the basic rule: if your competitors do it, don't do it. Be different. I did a seminar for a company sales team and they told me that they took their customers out to lunch as a thank you. I asked them what their competitors did to thank their customers and their reply was that they did the same as their competitors. I said to do something different to create a point of difference.

19. Establish your own V.I.P. club

Give your best customers a special discount or incentive card that they can present each time they buy your product. As a V.I.P. they may receive an additional bonus product, special offers or express service. Your customers will be appreciative of the extra recognition and V.I.P service. This is a great way to gain loyalty from your customers. If they are tempted to buy somewhere else, they will come back to you because of the additional bonuses or discount. I'm not a great believer in discounting, but I do believe in finding ways to create loyalty ideas that keep your customers coming back.

20. "How are things going?" customer calls

From time to time contact your customers by telephone, note or by fax just to see how they are going. It is a great way to stay in touch. An easy practical way is to use the alphabet to contact yourcustomers. Contact all the people starting with the letter "A" this week, all the people starting with "B" next week. In 26 weeks you will have contacted your entire database, which means your customers will have been personally contacted by you twice a year. You are not trying to sell them anything, but just touching base to say, "Hello and how are things going?"

21. Personal profile on each customer

It is important that you gain, not only the customer's business details, but also their personal preferences. There are a number of ways to capture your customer's details, from asking them, to having them complete a customer details card. Identify what you need to know, what you want to know for future reference, and the information on their buying habits that would assist you in planning for the future.

22. Conduct a regular customer survey

A great way to get feedback from your customers is to ask them for feedback through a survey. The majority of surveys don't have a high return rate.

One of the ways to get your customers to complete the survey and return it to you is to use a response tool. A response tool could be that the customers send the survey back by a certain time frame and they go into a prize draw.

Another may be to actually send the customers who complete the survey a product voucher to a certain value that they can use when they make their next purchase. This is a great way to have them keep coming back to your business.

An associate suggested we send a dollar scratchy ticket with the survey as a thank you in advance. Recently, we used the combination of the scratchy ticket and a prize draw. The results spoke for themselves.

Of the 270 surveys we sent out, 210 of them came back completed by the due date and 40 came back after the due date. A total of 250 surveys came back completed.

As a result of the two-page survey, which was both lead generating and the opportunity to gain some valuable feedback, we have enough advanced customer data to do our business market planning for the next two years.

Here is an example of a two-page survey. Once again, if you go to my website you can download this document and modify it to suit your purposes.

Name & Address

Hi (Name) ...

By the time it takes to hopefully scratch a fortune, you will have given us some feedback.

In the quest to build a better business, we know we need to strengthen our relationship with you, our client. To do this we need your feedback, suggestions, comments and thoughts. Listed below is a short questionnaire that will help us shape our business to meet your needs in the future.

Personal Details

Your e-mail Address;-................................. *Date of Birth ....*

Please indicate your favourite sport or hobby by ticking the circles below:

○ *Golf*	○ *Tennis*	○ *Boating*	○ *Fishing*
○ *Football*	○ *Horse Racing*	○ *Motor Racing*	○ *Movies*
○ *Arts*	○ *Theatre*	○ *Water Sports*	○ *Dining Out*
○ *Basketball*	○ *Polo*	○ *Reading*	
○ *Fine Wine*	○ *Other.*		

(Name), what's one thing you are passionate about?

....

Future planning

When will be your next purchase of our product/service?

○ *Last Quarter 1998* ○ *First Quarter 1999* ○ *Second Quarter 1999*
○ *Third Quarter 1999* ○ *Fourth Quarter 1999* ○ *Year 2000*

As you know we have built our business only from referrals. With this in mind, is there anyone else you know who would benefit from the services we provide? ***No/Yes, Please Call***

Newsletter feedback

Do you read our newsletter "The XYZ Report"? *Yes/No*

How would you best describe our newsletter?

1. It's a great read. I read it from cover to cover. ○
2. I like reading certain parts of your newsletter. ○
3. It's O.K. to read from time to time. ○
4. I don't read it at all. ○

Please use one or two words to describe its content or value.................................

Would you like some of your customers or associates to receive our newsletter with our compliments?
No/Yes, please call for their details.

WELL: In our business - what do we do really WELL which directly affects our business relationship regarding customer service, selling, marketing, or technical advice?

____

____

IMPROVE: In our business - what do you believe we need to improve upon so that we can service your needs better as a business and maximise our relationship in the future?

____

____

STRATEGY: Now that you have listed down what we need to improve upon, what steps do you suggest we take to ensure that these areas will be improved in the future?

____

____

ADDING VALUE: What else can we do to add value to your business and our business relationship? Our goal is to grow our business and to continue to be at the forefront of our industry. That's why it is important for us to be looking at ways to be of value to you.

____

____

(Customer's Name), thank you for taking the time to give us some valuable feedback. We appreciate your comments. We also know that to meet our customer's needs and to be able to continue to add value to your business, we need feedback. Now all you have to do is fax it back to us, on our 24-hour fax line (Your Fax Number).

Sincere Regards

(Your Name & Title)

P.S. *By faxing this feedback form back to us by the (Pick a date), you will go into the draw to win $XYZ of products.*

23. Read for your customers

From time to time you will read the newspaper, magazines, industry based publications and association newsletters. As you read these sources of information you may come across an article that relates to a particular customer or a group of your customers. The article may relate to their company, industry or one of their personal interests. Why not cut it out and send it to them with a short note, "I found this article. I thought it may be of interest to you." What would they think of you?

24. Sending positive faxes

If you are chatting with one of your customers and they are having a bad day or need a bit of a laugh, send them a positive fax with a motivational message on it or a funny cartoon. We all need a boost from time to time. As you well know, these are often the little things that count. It's not what you say, it's what you do that speaks volumes.

25. Gaining and using customer testimonials

It has often been said that you can promote anyone but yourself, because people don't listen to self-praise. If your customers promote you, then it must be the truth. Ask your customers to comment on the relationship they have with you, the service experience they received from you and your business, or why they like dealing with you. Have your customer write it down and forward it to you. You can then use these comments in your next brochure, in a poster, in your place of business or even as a supporting document with proposals or quotes.

I use customer testimonials in most of our presentation material. I even put testimonials with our proposals, with my customers name, title, company and contact phone number. I encourage my prospective customers to contact these people and ask them if I'm any good. I have received permission from my customers to do this. When the prospective customer contacts my customer they become an independent salesperson working with me.

A good time to ask for a testimonial is after the product has been delivered. During your follow-up sales call check if your customer is totally happy and satisfied. Once the customer has agreed to provide a testimonial you may want to fax them the letter below with these questions.

Once again, this letter is available on my website for you to download.

Date

Mr. John Smith
Manager
XYZ Company
45 Green Street
Brisbane. QLD. 4000.

Dear John,

Thank you, Thank you, Thank you.

Thank you for agreeing to write a short testimonial for me and thank you for agreeing to provide me with the names of some of your associates who can benefit from our services.

I know how hard it is to put pen to paper sometimes to write a testimonial. So I thought I would save you having to sit down and write a whole letter. I hope that's OK with you.

I have also given you some examples of what other people have written about our product and services as a guide for you.

If you know of anybody whom you think could benefit from our services, I have included some space for you to jot down their names. They may be associates from within your organisation or within your network of contacts.

All you need to do is to answer the five questions on the sheet attached and list the names, title, company and telephone numbers of your referrals. Then either send it back to me or fax it back on (01) 2345 6789 to our office. Simple and easy!

John, Thank you once again. I appreciate your cooperation and I look forward to working with you in the near future.

Sincere regards,

Peter Peterson
Manager

Thank you for your testimonial and referrals.

Listed below are five simple questions I would like you to answer. They won't take long to answer and the feedback will be of great value to our organisation.

1. *As a result of the product purchased, what have been the three major benefits your business has gained from our product?*

*a)*____

*b)*____

*c)*____

2. *How would you describe the service our people have given you during this service transaction?*

____

____

3. *In your opinion, how has our business added value to your business? Just jot down two lines, or some key phrases.*

____

____

4. *If you were going to refer our services and products to other business associates or to your network of contacts, what would you say about us and why they should use our services?*

____

____

5. *Please list three people who could benefit from the services we provide.*

Name	*Title*	*Company*	*Telephone*

Thank you for your time.

26. Write articles for your customer's newsletter or business publications

If you have ever written a newsletter you will know that it is often a hard task to get started, working out what to write each month or quarter. If your customers write a newsletter then this would be the same for them as well.

One way to add value to your customer and to enhance your profile within your customer's database, is to write a series of articles that relate to some topical generic issue or points of interest. If you have been writing your own newsletter for some time you may already have these articles sitting on your computer system. You may need to customise or modify them to suit the target audience for your customer's newsletter, but it would be time well spent.

I look at it this way, even if they don't take you up on your offer what would they think of you, because you offered? Would it set you apart from your competitors who do 2/5th of zip for them?

Make sure that the article is not about you. All you want in return is correct acknowledgment to be given for your contribution and the best way for the reader to contact you, if they have any questions. Make it an interesting read. To gain a greater response from your article, make a special offer for the reader.

27. Offer your speaking services to your customer's association

Some of your customers will belong to their industry-based association or local Chamber of Commerce. You may want to prepare a twenty-minute presentation about some of the changes affecting your industry or the seven technological advances your industry faces in the future. Make it interesting with facts, stories, real life examples and diagrams. Now I can hear you saying "I don't like to speak in public." This is a totally natural response as it has been recorded that public speaking is the second greatest fear known to man, only preceded by death. Of course you are not going to love every moment of it, but it is a great way to promote you and your business. You may want to offer your services to speak at your customer's staff conference to share your insights into the same topics or on how to work more effectively together to save time, money and energy.

28. Look to build strategic alliances with other service providers

You can add significant value to your customers through the quality of your professional network of contacts. The establishment of strategic alliances with other businesses could be of value and benefit to your customers. It could be just another way to strengthen the relationship with your customers.

Whom do you know that your customers could do business with? Are there other services or products that further complement your products or services? For example, if you own a hardware store, you could set up some strategic alliances with a landscape gardener, handyman, builder or electrician.

Perhaps you own a clothing store so you may want to set up a strategic alliance with an image consultant, hairdresser, gym or may be even a therapeutic masseur.

The key to this relationship is that it is a WIN/WIN/WIN relationship. It must be a win for you, for your strategic partner and most importantly, for your customer. Sometimes these relationships can be done on a straight referral basis, or even on some type of predetermined remuneration system. Once the alliance has been set up it is usually best to put it in writing so all parties know exactly what they have promised.

29. Set up a monthly hints and tips e-mail service

You may wish to put together a monthly, weekly or daily hints and tips program that, once again, adds value to your customers. It may be a business educational program where you give your customers five tips to improve customer service ideas; to market their products better; to make their product more productive or effective or you could include a positive thought-provoking quote. This process can be automated to save you time and energy. This could also be another service you offer to your customers free of charge.

30. Set up your own website - a customer service resource centre

This is a great opportunity to promote your services by setting up a question and answer section. Keep your site fresh with updated material. Provide articles of interest, free download, links with other sites that would add value to your customers. Your website can become a resource centre for your customers. Make your website, or certain parts of your website, for customers only and give your customers a special password. It communicates to them that they are an important part of your business and you value them.

31. Getting extra value from conferences or training seminar

From-time-to-time you will go to a conference or training seminar and pick up some great ideas that may be relevant to your customers. You may want to summarise some of these key ideas onto a sheet of paper and send them out with a note attached.

32. Don't send Christmas cards, send New Year's cards

How many Christmas cards did you receive last year? Who were they from? Who cares! Now don't misunderstand me, I am a great believer in the spirit of Christmas, but everyone sends Christmas cards. Now let me ask you, how many New Year's cards did you receive? The answer is probably "none".

Here is the point! If you want to create a point-of-difference that sets you apart, this is a great way to create that point, because not many people do it. If you are going to spend the same amount of money to carry out this activity, why not get a better result from your investment and efforts?

33. Either have a very early or a very late Christmas party

One of my customers has their Christmas party in February. That way they don't compete with other companies for the attention of their customers around the increasingly busy festive season. They even boast that they have become quite famous for their Christmas parties and normally get a near 100% customer attendance. Don't be scared to do things differently.

34. First day of Spring - send flowers

Send a flower, or flowers, to your key customers on the first day of spring with a note welcoming them to the next season and the next quarter of business activities. It may not be flowers, it could be flowers made out of chocolates, or flowers on a fax. Once again, I have seen this done by some of my customers with amazing results.

35. So many special days, so many opportunities to stay in contact

Look at the other times during the year when you can either write, send product offers or e-mail your customers on these special days; - Easter, Australia Day, Anzac Day, St. Patrick's Day, end of financial year, Valentines Day, Chinese New Year, Independence Day, Labour Day, Deepavali. This list is not complete. As you can see there are so many opportunities or reasons to communicate with your customers.

36. Make your own audio newsletter for your customers

A Brisbane-based organisation, McGirvan Media, produce their newsletter on audiotape. They interview successful business people from various industries with various points of view and ideas on how to be successful in the marketplace. They receive great feedback and have people lining up for this quarterly publication. If you want more information about this audiotape, or to receive a complimentary copy, you can access them through our website.

37. Audio tape as your business brochure

Have you ever thought about using your information, knowledge or expertise to create your own audiotape and provide it to your customers as a gift, or even use it as an additional product. The tape can be made up of hints and tips in an interview format where you have someone interview you. It could be about giving your customers inside knowledge on how to get the best results from some of your products.

38. Hints and tips booklet

I got this idea from an audiovisual hire company called "Staging Connections" who provide their customers with a small booklet about how to put together a great presentation; how to set up the room; how to use your audiovisual equipment, a check list of things to do before, during and after your presentation. It is a great reference booklet filled with valuable ideas. In the true concept of adding value this is a great way to do it. List down some of your secret hints and tips into a booklet for your customers to use. It may be a card you could laminate and put on five of your ideas, with your contact details.

39. Discount sticker on the customer's credit card

My wife and I went to a restaurant recently where we used our credit card. When the credit card receipt came back for me to sign, I noticed that there was a small sticker no bigger than the top of my little finger, with the name of the restaurant and the number 25 on it. When I asked the waitress about the sticker, she told me that next time I come back into the restaurant, I will get a 25% discount.

Now, I may not go back to that restaurant for some time but, every time I use my credit card, I think about that restaurant because of that red sticker. It's a great way of keeping them at the top of my mind because I am always using my credit card for business. A clever innovative idea!

40. Make luggage tags out of your customer's business cards

Once you have met someone, exchanged business cards and then placed their details into your database, what do you do with their business card? What we have been doing is taking the customer's business card, putting it into a special business card laminating pouch and running it through a laminating machine to transform it into a luggage tag for their briefcase.

We then send it back to them with a handwritten note. Taking this one step further, we glued another card on the back of their card before running it through the laminating process. On this card you may wish to put a positive quote or maybe offer a reward if the bag is ever lost, with your telephone number. Once again, it is something different. The feedback we have received has been very positive and it has won us a job valued at over $10,000.

41. Work in your customer's business

Take a couple of hours for either yourself, or some of your people, to work in your customer's business. Get to know what they do, how your product interfaces with their customers, learn about their challenges and how they run their business. By doing this your customer will appreciate you and see that you are committed to them and their people. You will also start to be treated like an asset to their business. This is the true essence of becoming a service partner. You would not do this with all your customers, but it is a practice worth implementing with your "A" customers.

42. Conduct training seminars for your customer's team of people

This is a great way to add value to your customer's business by educating their people. We live in the information age, so why not provide some additional information to assist your customer in their business and people in their roles within that business? The training sessions may be about your products and services, customer service skills or market trends that may affect their business in the future. Help your customers to equip their people for the future any they will consider you an asset to them.

43. Invite your customers along to other seminars

Another way to add value to your customers by furthering their education, is to invite them to other seminars. In your local area there are always a number of seminars being conducted. You make offer to take your customers along as a point of interest, or to get to know your customers on another level. These seminars may not have anything to do with your business or industry. These seminars may be run by different groups, Government bodies or the local Chamber of Commerce. You will find these seminars are generally inexpensive and great for networking. Even if your customer declines your invitation what will they think of you because you invited them?

44. Sponsored seminars for customers

You may want to think about conducting your own seminars. Find an appropriate speaker, an interesting relevant topic, invite some of your key customers, conduct it after work, and take this opportunity to equip your customers for the future. We have performed this activity for some of our customers with great success.

Heidelberg Australia and New Zealand have asked us to conduct a number of evening seminars for some of their best customers from the printing industry. Heidelberg specialise in manufacturing huge printing presses and digital imaging equipment worldwide. These seminars have nothing to do with Heidelberg or their equipment but they asked me to share a few loyalty concepts with their customers to help them become more profitable, and to work smarter in their tough marketplace. If you would like to know how these seminars can add value to your customer base, e-mail me at: passion@ppp.net.au and I will provide you with our seminar topics.

45. Footy tipping competition

A number of companies participate in footy tipping competitions, but what about running a separate competition for your key customers? What a great way to stay in touch with them every week. Put up a prize for that company or for the individuals who participate. Some of my customers do this each year and the feedback they get has been very positive. I also believe it will give you another opportunity to talk to them about something other than your product. *You should check with the lotteries division - you may need a permit.*

46. New customer functions

When any new relationship starts, it is always fragile. To build stronger relationships with your new customers you may want to conduct an after-hours function. You can tell them they are appreciated, show them around your business and introduce them to key people within your business. It is almost like an induction program for new customers. Lay a solid foundation from the start and your dealings with your customers will get easier as the relationship matures.

47. When your business wins an award

Often when businesses win an award which is service or industry related, they either tell no one about their success and recognition, or they go the whole hog and tell everyone about how great they are. I believe this is a great opportunity to say thank you to your customers for helping you achieve this honour.

A number of years ago Subaru won an Australian Car of the Year Award. Now, what most car manufacturers would do, is to tell everyone that they had just won this fantastic award; that they were great and that you and I should buy one of their award winning motor cars. Subaru did something very different. They took out full-page advertisements in most major newspapers saying thank you to all those people who had purchased one of their cars and made them so popular.

This campaign had a great impact with the public. Use the same principle in your business and take the opportunity to lift your credibility in your market place. Say thank you to your customers for helping you to achieve those awards or milestones. Remember your business would be out of business if you did not have loyal customers and, the last time I looked, I don't think they gave out awards to people who have gone out of business.

Well, there you have it, 47 ideas to help you create loyal profitable customers. I often say good ideas and good intentions are worth nothing unless you implement them into your business to maximise your true business potential. Not every idea will be applicable to your business, so take the ones that are and implement them now.

See our web page for online courses to be able to receive some of the world's best customer loyalty ideas on a continual basis. I have set up this special "Leading edge loyalty ideas" electronic coaching program to keep you on track. With this program, each week you will receive from me one personalised e-mail with a leading edge customer loyalty idea and how to implement it into your business.

All you have to do is visit my website at http://www.ppp.net.au log on and use the following password: Loyal Customers.

You, like most of my customers from time to time, will come across some great customer loyalty ideas. If you would like to share those with other business people, you can e-mail them to my office at:passion@ppp.net.au or fax them to me at: 61.07.3892 7493 or phone our office on 61.07.3848 5646. If I publish your ideas I will be sure to give you credit for them and I would also like to reward you for your efforts, so please ensure you give me your name, business name, address and contact number.

Chapter 6 - Practical business projects

Please identify what loyalty building ideas you could use in your business.

Chapter 7 – People

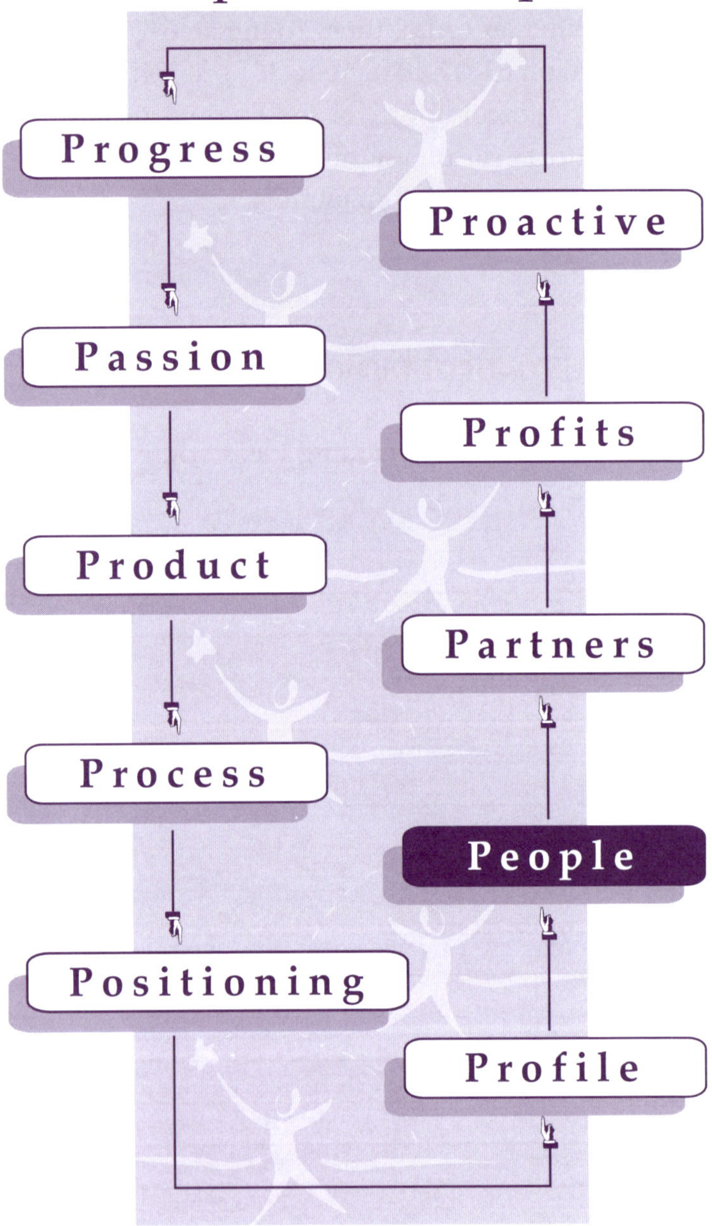

Creating Loyal Profitable Customers

PEOPLE

Are your people focused on what really counts?

"People who perform with a passion, produce productive results on a consistent basis."

Your business would be pretty boring if you had no people working in it. Now before you say "but I would have a lot less hassles", think about it this way, your customers do business with people, not a product. Once you have developed your product to be consistent, then you need to work on your people. How many of us have been consistently inconsistent, instead of being consistently consistent in our businesses?

If our people are not equipped and don't know how to follow in our footsteps then that is not their fault. It is ours for not training them to help us leverage our time. You see, we need to give our people a reason to follow and to contribute to our business in a positive way. If we don't, we start to feel the burden of sole responsibility which may weigh us down in our day-to-day business dealings. The critical factors here are: ensuring we have the right people with the right goals, running on the right track. The model (on the following page) is designed to help managers and leaders become better coaches.

Right People - Right Goals - Right Track Right Results Model

Focus your people on the right goals

For your people to follow you in your business they need both a long-term vision and short-term goals to follow. If you are the leader of your business, blazing this new path, and no one is following you, then you are just out taking a walk. Now, before you tell me that you told your people this at this year's annual conference or at last month's team meeting and everyone knows the direction you are going in the next twelve months, go and ask your people to articulate your goals. The results will surprise you.

70% to 80% of people would not be able to tell you in a clear and concise manner your goals or current direction. Now it's not their fault, we all get busy being busy and as you know, goal setting is easy. It's remaining focused on these goals that is the hard part.

Here are 5 things you can do to reinforce your goals with your people.

1. Every time you have a meeting or team get together talk about your goals and your progress.

2. Get your people involved in the goal setting or business planning process. By doing this you will get them to take ownership of your goals. As a team they will no longer be your goals but will become their goals.

3. Get your people to identify what they are going to do to contribute to those goals this month or week.

4. Keep your long-term and short-term goals in front of your team members, on the staff notice board or company newsletter.

5. Reward progress, improvements and achievements within your team and compliment those people who contributed to your goals.

Ownership - If your people own the business goals, they will face the challenges, they will find the solutions and they will share the successes.

Recruit the right people to achieve the right goals

Just as we profiled the right customer for your business in a previous chapter, we need to identify what the right person is for your business to achieve the right results. What type of people do you need in your business now? This process is vital for the long- term longevity of your business.

Here are a number of steps to take to get the right people working for you.

- Review your overall business goals to identify where you will need assistance in the future.
- Look at the people you currently have in your team and ask yourself "Are they the best people for the job?"
- Design a profile of the best person for the job. What skills do they have? What level of knowledge do they have? What type of qualities or characteristics do they demonstrate? Where would you find these people? What would be the best way to recruit them?
- Who in your team needs additional training and development to assist in bringing their potential into reality?

Develop your people to achieve the right results

As the leader of your business you need to equip your people with skills, knowledge and with the right attitude to achieve the results your business requires for its long- term competitiveness. People are always the unknown factor in any business equation. Your role as owner or leader is to equip them to produce the best results. If you don't do it, then who will? If it's not you, then who? If it's not now, then when?

Plant seeds today to equip yourself for tomorrow, and you never have to worry about the future again.

Here are some ways to equip your people to achieve in your ever-changing business environment.

- Set up your own corporate library of tapes, books and videos for your people to access.
- Employ people who believe in ongoing self-development.
- Provide training sessions that not only relate to their role, but also enhance their own personal growth.

- Set up a program where people get the opportunity to work with other people in your business or your customer's business. This will assist with multi-skilling as well as the internal and external relationship building.
- Establish relationships with learning organisations, so that your people can access their materials, programs and resources with ease.
- Encourage your people to learn about technology, global business trends and marketplace changes, so that they have a bigger picture of the marketplace.
- Support your people by assisting them to get involved with industry-based associations and organisations.

EQUIP - **E**ncouraging **Q**ualities **U**ndeveloped **I**n **P**eople.

John Maxwell - Author of "Developing the Leader Within"

Reward and recognise your people's achievements

I read a statistic that said the number one reason why people left their job was because of a lack of recognition and the number ten reason was that they were not suitably remunerated within their role. I don't know about you, but that tells me that people will go the extra mile in your business, if you recognise them sincerely on a regular basis. They may not expect a pay raise every time they do something right, but they do expect a thank you or a job-well-done comment.

Always remember what gets rewarded, gets repeated.

I once used this approach when I was a manager of a large team of people. Their staff turnover rate was just over 100% and we had to work together to achieve an annual budget of $15,000,000. I noticed the previous management team always found their people to be doing something wrong. I decided if I was going to turn the business around, to achieve our budget and stop staff turnover, a different approach was needed.

I went out and found people doing things right and I recognised them for that and for the extra effort people were putting in. It worked really well. In actual fact, it was easier to discipline people when they did the wrong thing because it was fair.They got feedback when it didn't work and praise when it did work. In a three month period we stopped staff turnover altogether and became the number one area in Australia.

Here are some ways to encourage and recognise your people:

- Set up a team and an individual recognition system, so that you have the flexibility to give praise for the appropriate effort.
- Get people within your team to give praise and recognition.
- Change your recognition system around on a regular basis so that people don't get bored with it.
- Take the time to write thank-you notes to people for the extra effort. A little bit of ink goes a long way.
- Set up a business environment where it is OK to have fun, to make mistakes as long as people learn from them and to achieve, as they work together as a team.

Coach your key people to lead your business

If you cannot pass the leadership role onto someone in your team then you don't own your business, the business owns you. Not everyone in your team needs to be developed into a leader. You need to have a person to take your place, to succeed you in your role.

One of the keys to business leverage is being able to take a step back to work on your business. If you cannot do this because you are too involved in your business, then you need to find someone to give you back that time.

I see it so often in business. This person builds a great business because they are good at servicing the customers, building relationships and relating to the customer's needs. But because their business has grown they are now stuck doing the paper work and not dealing with the customer.

Why? Because they do not have the time anymore! Find the right people with the right goals and right systems to support them and it will give you back time.

By cloning yourself with another leader, you can start to take your business to the next level. What I'm saying is you not only have got to be the manager and the leader of your business, but also the coach of your key people.

The Business leader coaching formula consists of:

1. *Clearly defined direction*

Your key people need to know where they are going and be working towards their key performance indicators. You may need to review these on a regular basis to assess their progress and achievements.

2. Attitude check up

The attitude we look for in key people to develop is one that is solution-focused.They have a positive attitude, a "can do" mind set, someone who is teachable and someone who is prepared to contribute to your team.

3. Skills and knowledge checkup

Have your key people got the basic skills and knowledge to work with? Are they prepared to learn? Where are the skill or knowledge gaps with your key people? At the end of the day skills and knowledge can be acquired if people want to learn. If they can see the benefit to themselves, their role and to their customers, they will be motivated to learn.

4. Make Agreements to Follow-Up

People get excited and enthused about becoming a leader or taking on a bigger role within your business.Your goal as the leader is to ensure that this energy is followed through with action.What gets measurement gets maintained.Your role as the leader is to follow up with your people. If your people commit to a certain plan of action, then you need to follow it up at a later date.

What gets measurement gets maintained.

5. Equipping strategies

Spend time with your people to equip them to do your role. Get good at delegating the correct way. I like what Stephen Covey said, "Give a man a fish and you feed him for a day.Teach a man to fish and you feed him for a lifetime." Our role is to develop our people, lead by example, not just by verbal diarrhoea.The faster you develop your team members, the faster the principle of synergy is created. Remember, the speed of the business is the speed of the leaders.

If you don't grow as individuals in your business, your business will not go to the next level. You must grow them mentally, before you can go there physically.

6. *Positive business environment*

The culture you create is critical for everyone in your team, but more so for the key people that make up your leadership team. Think about what you are trying to create within your business. What do you stand for as a business? Is it OK for people to make mistakes as long as they learn from them? If they are not enjoying themselves, there is a fair chance the customer won't either. It is about creating the great unmeasurable but the totally identifiable - "team spirit".

"People are developed the same way gold is mined. Several tons of dirt must be moved to get an ounce of gold. But you don't go into the mine looking for dirt. You go in looking for gold!"

Andrew Carnegie

Chapter 7 - Practical Business Projects

Please answer the following questions to assist you in identifying who you need to work with to create great leaders in your business.

1. What are the profiles of the people you need, to be able to take your business to the next level in your marketplace?

____

____

____

____

2. What skills or knowledge do you provide to your people to equip them for the future marketplace you wish to compete in?

____

____

____

____

3. What type of business environment do you need to create to ensure that your customers receive an exceptional service experience?

____

____

____

____

4. What recognition systems have you got in place to ensure that you reward outstanding customer service given by your people?

____

____

____

____

5. Whom have you identified as potential leaders for your business in the future?

____

____

____

____

____

6. What do you do to equip and develop your key people in your business, so that they can become great business leaders?

____

____

____

____

____

Chapter 8 – Partners

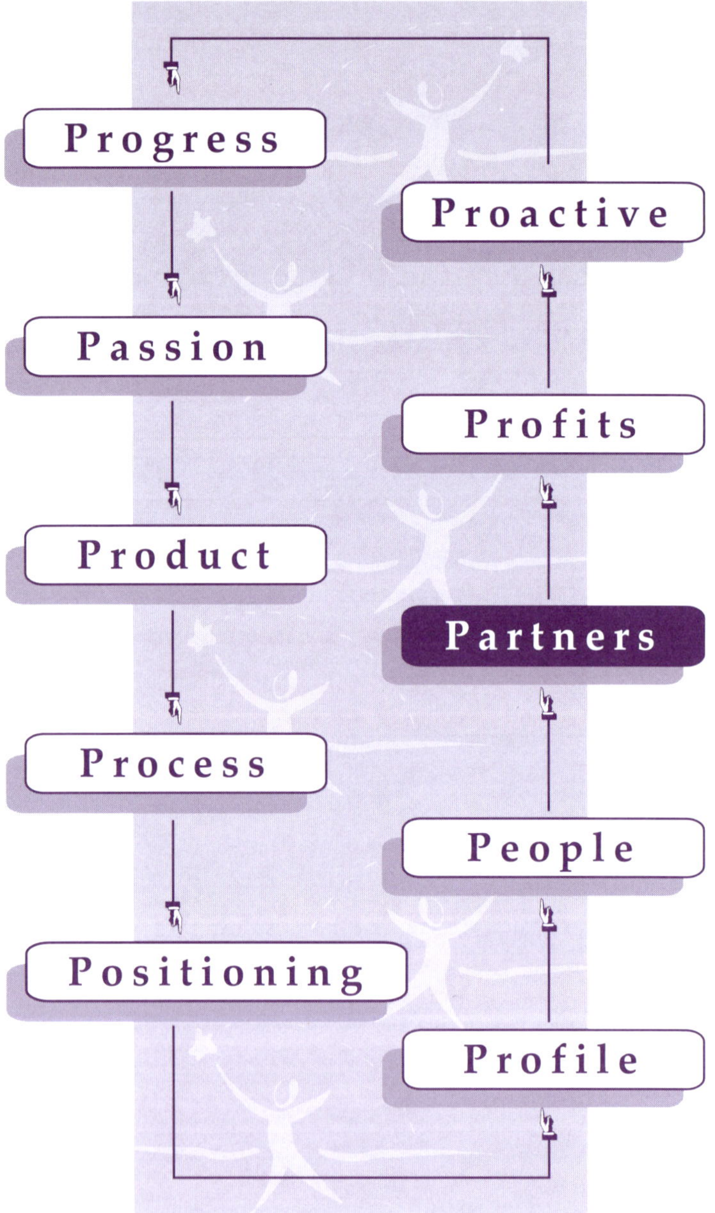

Creating Loyal Profitable Customers

Build strategic alliances that add value to your customers

"Look to build a personal and professional network that enhances the relationships of all parties - you, your customer and your associates"

I believe that the value of your business will not only rest on what your business turns over, but also on the quality of the contacts that make up your personal and professional network. I think we all know the saying, "It's not what you know, but whom you know". I think in these competitive times we live in, we need to have both, the knowledge and the network.

WIN/WIN/WIN relationships

You have probably seen the management catch cry of WIN/WIN relationships. However, when you start talking about setting up strategic alliances, the relationship you want to establish needs to add value not only to your customers, but also to your strategic partner, and, of course, your business in the process. So often I see strategic partnerships start and it's just a win for the business and for the strategic partner, not for the customer.

Always put yourself in each person's shoes and ask yourself the following:

- Is this a good deal for my business?
- Will this relationship comprise of anything I am looking to create in the future?
- Will my customers believe this to be of great value and enough to prompt a favourable response?

- Will it benefit my strategic partner, either from a marketing or sales point of view?

What is a strategic alliance?

Strategic alliances can come in all shapes and sizes.They can be for a set period of time or for an ongoing basis. Here are some of the examples of some obvious strategic alliances:

- A builder who renovates homes may have a strategic relationship with plumbers, electricians and landscape gardeners. He may also have a relationship with an architect or an interior designer to ensure the customer gets the right image all the way through the project.
- An accountant may have a strategic alliance with a solicitor, finance broker, insurance broker, financial planner, investment property expert and a stockbroker.All of these people's services cross one another and can add value to the accountant's customer at some stage.
- A veterinarian who specialises in horse care may have a solid relationship with the produce storeowner, a blacksmith, horse breaker and the company that services horse floats.
- A management consultant could team up with a human resources specialist or a marketing guru to be able to reposition that particular business or a financial expert to restructure the business financially.
- A recruitment specialist could have someone give their client advice on the clothes to wear, where to update their wardrobe or set up a strategic alliance with a computer college to help that person update their technology skills so they are more employable.

These are very obvious strategic alliances. However, the partnerships may not always seem so obvious at the time. Some of your short-term alliances may not have a direct relationship with your product.

It could be something that builds credibility or rapport with your customers. For instance, perhaps you own a mobile car repair business but one of your associates has a lawn mowing franchise. There is no direct relationship with a car repairer and having your lawn mowed. However, both sets of these businesses have customers who may need both services from time to time. The mobile repair business could hand out a half-price lawn mowing voucher and the lawn mowing person could hand their customers a free oil change voucher when the customer has their brakes checked. It's all about WIN/WIN/WIN.

How do you identify your strategic partners?

Sometimes you need to think outside the box. Here are some questions to think about when you want to identify your key strategic partners:

- Does this strategic partner have the same ethics and service standards as my business? In other words, will they honour their promises?
- What products or services would complement the services and products I have on offer?
- Who in my local area or my customer's demographic area would be the best business to approach?
- What products or services do my customers use on a regular basis in their business or personal lives?
- Whom do I know that would be able to provide these products or services reliably to my customers?
- Would the proposed strategic alliance partner's customers benefit from my products or services?
- What do I want to gain from this strategic alliance? Is it greater exposure to their marketplace? Is it additional prospects or leads? Is it a profiling exercise, or is it to generate more bottom line sales?

How to establish a strategic alliance relationship

Like any relationship, a strategic alliance needs to be built on trust ensuring there is mutual benefit. Once you have identified the businesses you want to build a relationship with, you need to go about the process of building the relationship. It may be through your centres of influence or by obtaining a referral from an existing customer. You want to start off with some type of reference point like a referral. If you cannot get a referral then you could make a cold call and set up a meeting.

During that phone call you want to paint a picture of what you are trying to establish with their business. You may want to talk about the benefits to their business and the benefits to your customers. You could send them some information about who you are and what you do. Then give them a follow up-call to answer any questions and to set up a time to get together to discuss your proposal further. What you are trying to do during this period of time is build up your credibility and trust with that person.

When you go to that meeting be prepared. Go there with a clearly defined goal, an agenda for the meeting. Have your questions written out and make sure that you outline the benefits to them, their customers, your customers and your business. Once an agreement has been reached, then the logistics of implementing or introducing this new alliance to all parties is critical. Remember the devil is in the detail. Gain agreement, document the agreement, sign off on the agreement and then follow through with your agreements.

Introducing your new strategic alliance

There are a number of ways to introduce your alliance. When we set up our strategic alliance with McGirvan Media we wrote to our customers with a copy of their quarterly audio newsletter and an offer. It went something like this:

If you want to continue to receive this audio newsletter just simply contact the McGirvan office and they will continue to send it to you with our compliments and that of McGirvan Media.

What I did was contribute to that newsletter in the form of an interview with Alan McGirvan. He gave his listeners a special offer on the audiotape for some free additional information relating to the topic I spoke about. It was a win for everyone!

Here are a couple of ways to introduce your new alliance to your customers:

- It could be through a letter, fax or e-mail letting your customers know about the alliance. You may want to attach a special offer that would guarantee a positive response. Make this offer very inviting and have a timeframe for acceptance.
- You may want to invite some of your best customers and some of their best customers to a function. Have a small presentation that gives an overview of each business and once again make an offer on the night to entice the customers to try your product or service. This function can be conducted as two separate functions, where you speak to their customers at one function and, on another night, they speak to your customers.
- It could be as simple as giving out vouchers for your strategic partner's services and products and they reciprocate. Work out the cost of getting a new customer in your business, how much it costs you in advertising, time and energy. Then take that dollar and use it as the dollar basis to develop an offer for your strategic partner's customers, for example, if it costs you $10.00 to get a new customer to walk into your door and you work on a 100% markup and your least expensive product is $10.00, then your offer may be between $10.00 and $15.00. Your offer may be, if a customer spends over $50.00 they will receive a free $10.00 gift or a $10.00 discount. You work out the best offer for your business and marketplace.

Build your network to build your business

Networking is vital in today's business world. You and I need to take time to build our personal and professional networks. As a result of this networking some great strategic alliances will come to the forefront. Now I mean real networking. That's where you get up and go and meet other people, where you extend your hand first to introduce yourself, to find out what people do, how they do it and whom they do it for.

Often I get invited to go along and speak at networking breakfasts or lunches and watch as everyone arrives. They come in and sit down, have their meal, listen to the speaker and all they have done is met the person either side of them. That's only a small part of networking.

Here are some strategies that have worked for me when I network.

- Think about the questions you can ask people when you meet them. Ask them what work they do, who they do it for and where they do it. Be prepared to be interested in people and they will become interested in what you do in your business.
- Always have your business cards on you or very close by. I always carry my business cards in my diary, wallet, business folder and car. It always makes me laugh when I ask for someone's business card and they say, "I haven't got any on me. They are back in my office." I think to myself, "you don't need to meet anyone else in your office, they already know you".
- Turn your business card into a memorable document. Use the back of your card to tell people what you do and the benefits of using your products and services. You may want to put your photo on your card. My card is a two-fold mini brochure. My mates tell me it looks like my first book published. It has quotes on it, tells people what I do and it makes people think. People always make positive comments about my business card, which makes it memorable.

- This may be a simple one, but always carry a pen with you. The amount of salespeople who don't carry them amazes me. What if you are given a great referral or discover an excellent opportunity for your product or service and cannot write it down. A couple of notes on the back of their business card may help you remember them. If you are like me, I think of an idea as I'm driving along. If I don't write it down, two traffic lights later I can't remember what it was.
- Write notes to people after you meet them and make sure you include your business card. Be different and set out to make a point-of-difference.
- Get yourself involved with some positive, proactive networking organisations such as Rotary, Apex, Lions, SWAP, Leads clubs, Chamber of Commerce, industry based associations or local business clubs. You may even want to set up your own local unofficial networking group with some like-minded people.

If you want to get a better understanding of networking, then keep a look out for one of the world's foremost experts and author of 'Networking Magic' and her first book - 'Be Seen, Get Known and Move Ahead,' Robyn Henderson. Robyn can be contacted on (02) 9369 1025 or inetwork@ozemail.com.au.

Take the hard road now

Strategic alliances are a great way to add value to your business and your customers. They are an excellent way to leverage your time in your business through other channels and networks. The opportunity is there to make it work for you. All you need to do is spend the time to set it up. I always like that quote, "If you keep on taking the easy road it will eventually get harder, but if you take the hard road now it will eventually get easier." Building strategic alliances is the hard road, but it will make your business life so much easier.

Chapter 8 - Practical business projects

The following questions will assist you in clarifying whom you can network with to establish positive strategic alliances for your customers to benefit.

1. Who do you know that could add value to the products and services your customers purchase from you?

2. What's the best way to approach those people to set up a strategic alliance?

3. What would be the best way to promote this new strategic alliance to your customer base?

4. What organisations do you need to research to enhance your network of contacts?

"The strength of your business in the future will be gauged by the quality of the strategic alliances you have developed."

Chapter 9 – Profits

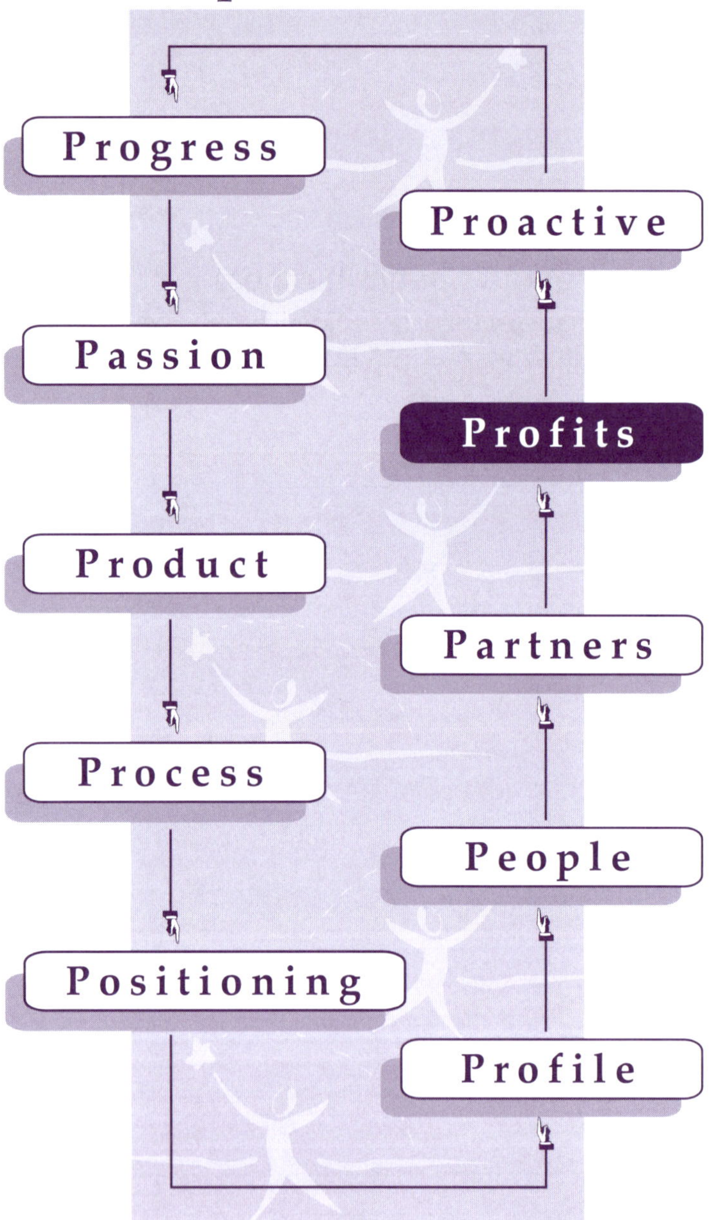

Creating Loyal Profitable Customers

PROFITS

At the end of the day are you making profits?

"You are either in business to make a profit or you will go out of business as an unregistered charity."

I think in business we can all appreciate the difference between "gross and net income", and if we don't, we soon will be out of business. As I have mentioned in a previous chapter, one of the key ways to build a profitable business is to control your expenses by looking at ways to drive them down, but not to the detriment of your business. I have seen quite a number of businesses which were trimmed to the backbone and could not function. I like what Tom Peters said about business, "You can't shrink your way to greatness, you have to grow there".

Working for profitability in your business

There are only three broad areas to look at when you want to enhance the profitability of your business. In this chapter my goal is to make you think, to confirm that you are on the right track with the current profitability plan you have in place for your business. You need to:

- Look at ways to drive down your business expenses
- Maximise the opportunities in your customer base
- Be creative in finding ways to work smarter

As a friend of mine said recently, "What are you focused on - gross or net income?" There is always a way to make your business more profitable. It is up to you to find the ways even though you may have explored every possible way for your business to be more profitable six months ago. That was six months ago. Today there could be some new technology or concept available or different process for you to use in the quest for greater profitability.

Look at ways to drive down your business expenses

Identify every expense that your business has, both fixed or variable. Then identify in which areas you waste money. Look at the areas you could save money in if you were to work more effectively. Check these expenses against your budgeted amount and then go back regularly to make sure you are on target. You can lose control of your profitability plan if you don't focus on these small numbers. It is sometimes the small expenses where you can save the most dollars.

Look at the hidden costs in your business e.g. the cost of replacing people if someone leaves; the dollars wasted in unproductive time when you have to up-skill that new person; a piece of equipment that breaks down on a regular basis; or a piece of equipment that does not work effectively and costs you time or frustration because of its output. Look at any process in your business where you waste time, money or there is a frustration factor attached to it. The frustration factor has an impact on you and your people, which could be affecting productivity.

More importantly when you look at your expenses, involve all the key stakeholders, such as your accountant, accounts department or maybe even the staff across your organisation. These people may have some great ways to save you money that may have been over looked because you were too close to your business.

Recently I took a step back and looked at some of our processes to identify ways to work smarter and to save money as well.

Here are some of the ways we thought of for our business, to save time and money:

- Start sending invoices via e-mail.
- Put logistic sheet with all of my requirements for when I speak at conferences on our Website so people can download them.
- I'm often asked for my biography and photo for conference promotional brochure. Once again this can be put on the Website for customers to access.
- Use E-tickets when travelling as it saves having to line up twice, once to get the ticket and once to check in.
- Have our customers deposit our fees straight into our bank account. It saves standing in line at the bank.
- Do more telephone banking, save having to go to the bank at all.
- Check out all the different long distance, fax and mobile telephone plans that are available and make sure we are on the right plan for our business and usage.
- Identify the areas where we have high expenditure and consider doing a twelve month deal with some service providers based on last year's spending with them.

These were just some of the ideas we came up with in a 15-minute brainstorming exercise. Think about it for your business and personal expenditure.

Maximise the opportunities in your customer base

You could be sitting on a goldmine with your customer base. How many of your customers use only one of your products instead of the whole range? The opportunities to cross sell or up sell additional products to your customers is one way to grow your business and make yourself more profitable. We will be showing you how to do this by using a multiplying formula (on the following pages).

Let's look at the three key aspects of your business. Firstly, the number of customers that do business with you. Secondly, the number of transactions they do with your business in a set period of time and thirdly, the average amount of money they spend with you each time they do business. Let's play with some numbers to show you the power of the multiplying formula in business.

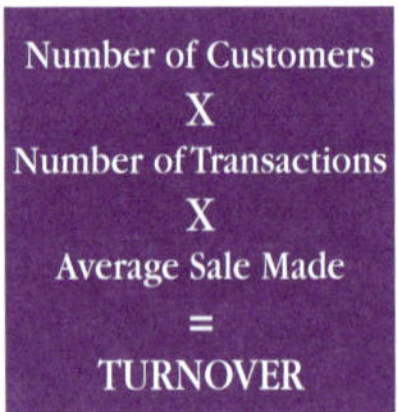

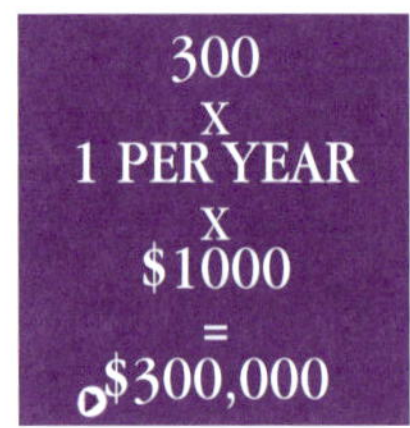

In this business the owners will turn over **$300,000** for the year. But if we use the multiplying factor, that is, we increase each of these three areas by say 20%, all of a sudden we have a compounding effect without a massive amount of effort. Let's now look at the numbers:

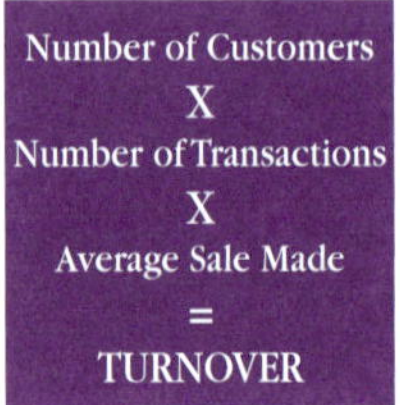

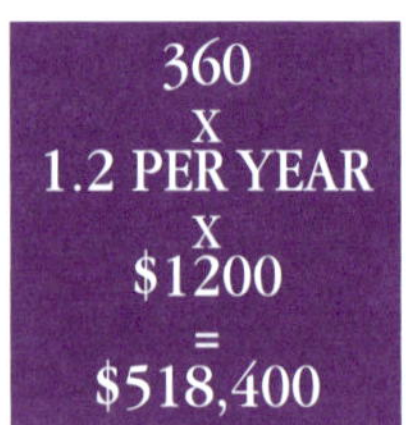

This business now turns over **$518,400** for the year. That's almost double the turnover without double the effort. But what normally happens in business is you want to grow your business, so you go out and find more customers. Now that is O.K., but you need to work on the other areas at the same time. Instead of just putting in a referral program or a new advertising campaign, think about how you can get your customers to spend more with you through the introduction of other products and services. Think about the ways to get some of your customers to make additional purchases in your business.

Maybe, it's not 20% across the board. You may not be able to increase the customers by 20%; maybe it is only 10%. Perhaps you can increase the number of transactions by 50% and the average amount spent with you by 30%. What does that look like now?

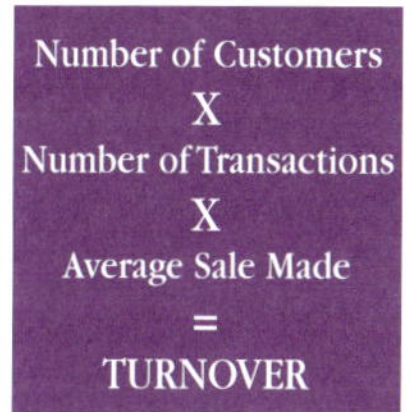

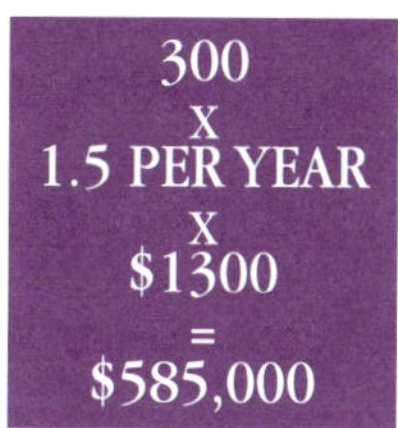

The business turnover is now **$585,000**. You can play with the numbers for your own business. This is a great exercise to do when you next think about how you are going to increase your turnover. Once you have done the numbers you need to think about the strategies you are going to use to influence your customers in these three areas. Broadly speaking each of these three areas can be influenced by the quality of customer loyalty you have. By developing a frequent contact program you increase your chances of gaining more referrals, more sales from customers who buy from you more often. Work on the numbers for yourself. You will be surprised.

As I have mentioned before the ability to cross sell your products is one way to improve your turnover and profitability. Cross selling is where your customers buy one of your products and you offer another product or service in the range that would complement that product purchased. With very little effort you get an additional sale and that is smart business. But how often do your customers come into your business and buy one product and then go down the road and buy another product you stock from your competitor, because you never asked the question or promoted another one of your products or service.

Here are some basic rules to follow when you and your people cross sell.

- Everyone needs good product knowledge, in order to promote the right product to the customer. In other words, what product goes with what product in your business?
- People need to cross sell all the time and make it a habit. You need to have a focus on a particular product each month if necessary.

- You and your people need to understand that cross selling is nothing more than offering other alternatives and options to your customers. Think of it as a different service.

- Give your customers a reason why you are recommending an additional product or service.

- Ask good quality questions to understand the customer's needs and take note when they tell you about other opportunities where you can offer other product options.

- Everyone needs to know the cross selling phrases to lead your customer smoothly into a cross selling opportunity. Such as:

  - *Is there anything else I can assist you with today?*
  - *You mentioned that your video isn't working. Is it important to you to get it working or to replace it at the moment?*
  - *Can I suggest that you look at the next model up?*
  - *Are you also aware that we provide an installation service for that product?*
  - *I notice that you have been using ABC Shampoo. Could I recommend this new XZY All In One Shampoo & Conditioner?*

Be creative in finding ways to work smarter

I think we all work hard but do we work smart? Take a step back from your business and ask yourself these questions:

- Where in our business can we save money?
- Where in our business do we waste money?
- Where in our business do we waste time?
- Where in our business can we save time?
- How do we make our people more productive?
- Where do my people waste time and money?
- What roadblocks have we put in front of our people that stop them from working more effectively?
- What processes could enhance our service selling experience?
- What would be a better way to advertise or promote ourselves in our market place?
- Is there a better way to distribute our products and services to our customers?
- How do we improve our cash flow situation?
- What can we do to improve morale, motivation and business momentum?
- Who can I set up a strategic alliance with to add value to what we do for our customers?

- What products can we cross sell to our customers to maximise our customer base?

Maybe you are not the best person to answer these questions. It could be that you are too close to your business which means that your opinion may be one-sided or your mind may be stuck in the business rut. Don't be afraid to ask your people, other business associates, customers or friends to help you answer these questions. The responses could be a pleasant surprise because the answer was so obvious.

Chapter 9 - Practical business projects

Please answer the following questions to assist you in making your business even more profitable in the future.

1. Where in your business do you waste time and money?

____

____

____

____

2. What could you do to make your people more productive in the future?

____

____

____

____

3. What products or services could you be promoting in your business as a cross selling opportunity?

____

____

____

____

4. How do you use the multiplying factor to grow your business?

____

____

____

____

5. What can you do to influence the three parts of the multiplying factor, the number of customers, the number of transactions and the average amount of money they spend in your business?

____

____

____

____

Chapter 10 – Proactive

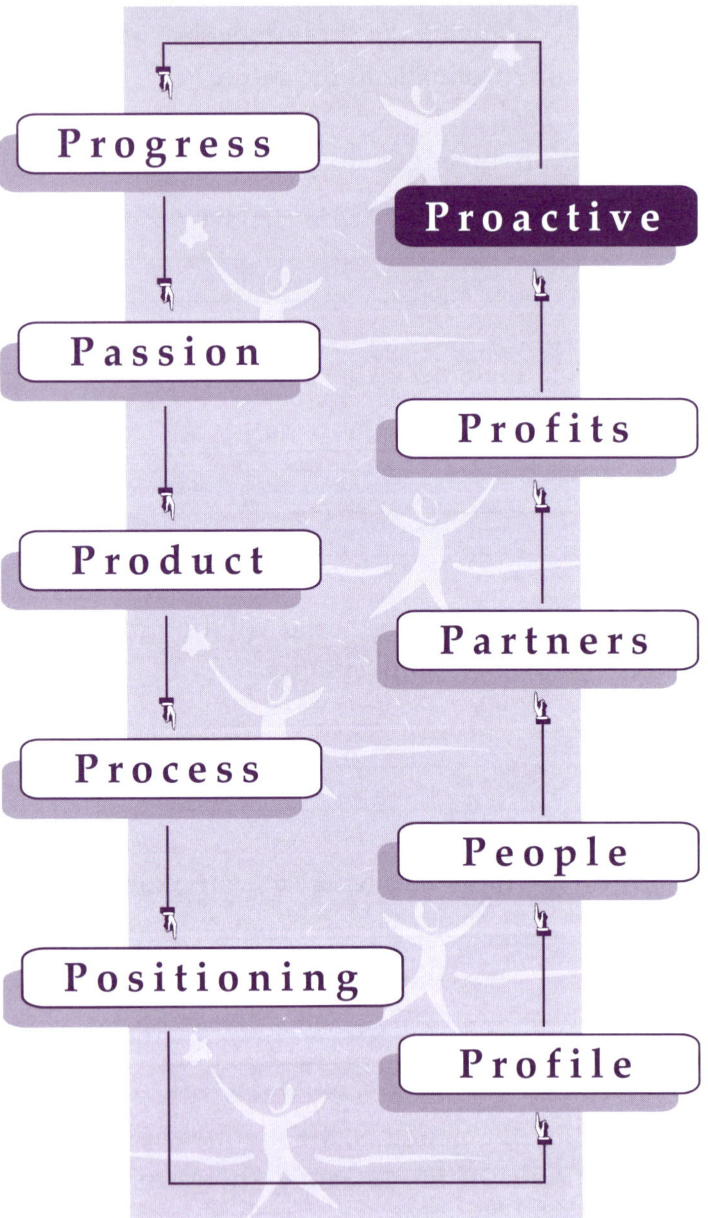

Creating Loyal Profitable Customers

PROACTIVE

It's not what you say that counts; it's what you do that makes the difference

"How you respond to the challenge in the second half, will determine what you become after the game. Whether you are a winner or a loser."

Lou Holtz

I always think it's not what you say you are going to do but what you actually do that determines the character of a person. Regardless of where you have come from, you can always come back to achieve your true potential. Thank you for taking the time to invest in your personal and professional development. For you and I our constant challenge will be what to do today for our future. Good ideas and good intentions don't amount to much without action.

Plant seeds today that will equip you for tomorrow and you will never have to worry about the future again.

There are three ways to look at the future. You can be reactive to it, which means you are always behind and never in control of your future direction. You could be adaptive, where you are making some progress with some control, but you have to look hard to see if you are moving in the right direction. Then you could choose to be proactive. When you are in control of your plans for the future, things will happen.

Reactive ⟶ **Adaptive** ⟶ **Proactive**

Where To Now?

So what is next for you? Are you going to be proactive? If the answer is yes, then can I strongly suggest you identify the five critical things you need to do now to gain greater customer loyalty. Don't pick 101 different ideas to work on, just pick five to begin with. They may not be big ideas, but by completing them you will start to gain momentum in your business towards your desired outcomes. These ideas will assist you to move through these changing times.

Definition of Insanity - Keep on doing what you always have but expecting a different result. That will drive you insane.

I read a story once that said, if you want to stop a train from moving, you put a block of wood in front of it which will stop it from moving. But if that train is travelling at 60 kilometres an hour, fifteen feet of reinforced concrete won't stop it. What's the difference between the two trains? One has momentum. If you gave me a choice between momentum and motivation for my business, I would take momentum every time. Pick five ideas from this book that are going to give you and your business some fabulous momentum. Write them down.

1.____

2.____

3.____

4.____

5.____

The question is when are you going to complete these five tasks? What I know from personal experience is that if my goals are vague, so are my results! Set a deadline for when you are going to have these tasks completed. Make sure you have a start date and a completion date.

The ideas don't stop here - enrol in our weekly loyalty message program!

I have set up special online courses on our Website http://www.ppp.net.au.

This book may have created more questions than answers for you. If you have a question just e-mail me and I will respond to you.

3% of people make things happen!
10% of people expect things to happen!
60% of people just watch things happen!
27% of people don't know what happened!

Which category are you going to fall into?

Plant seeds today, knowing you won't reap a reward from them today

A story was once told to me about a young English boy who went swimming on his father's country estate. If you could picture the setting; it was a lovely warm summer's day, not a cloud in the sky. The boy's family, who were very wealthy owned this magnificent estate with beautiful gardens which surrounded a picturesque lake. The boy decided that today was a great day to go swimming. So he took off his robe, tightened his bather's cord and dived into the water.

He was having a great time swimming and playing in the lake. As time when by, he became more and more adventurous. As he tired he noticed he had gotten into water too deep for his swimming ability. He panicked and started to call for help. Alongside the lake, attending to some flowers and shrubs, was the estate's resident gardener. Hearing the boy's cries for help he downed his tools and dived into the water without a moment's hesitation. The gardener got to the boy and had him safely ashore in no time.

By this time the boy's father had turned up to help. The boy's father, as you could imagine, was beside himself. He was deeply indebted to his gardener for saving his son's life. As a sign of goodwill, the boy's father asked the gardener what he could do to repay the debt. The gardener, who was a modest man, said, "I don't want anything, sir. You gave me a job, when I needed one, you feed my family and you put a roof over our head. I don't want anything from you". The boy's father persisted. "There must be something I can do for you to repay your efforts in saving my son's life?"

The gardener thought for a moment, then said, "Sir I have a son. He is only three years old. I don't know what he wants to be but I would like him to have an education. Your son will go to the some of the best schools in England. I would like my son to have an opportunity to go to school." The boy's father responded by saying, "I will sponsor your son's education. If he wants to go to school I will pay for it. Even if he wants to go to university, I will pay for that as well." The agreement was sealed with a handshake.

The boy who was saved that day grew up to become one of England's finest statesmen and Prime Ministers. His name was Sir Winston Churchill. During his Prime Ministership, Sir Winston became very ill. His personal assistant was sent to find the best doctor in England. He found a fellow called Sir Alexander Fleming. He was the gardener's son.

I thought this true story was appropriate to make the point that we need to plant seeds today but that we may not reap the reward today. But I can guarantee you this; if you plant no seeds you will reap no rewards.

I hope during this book I have given you a number of ideas that will make a difference. Finally, thank you and I leave you with this verse to ponder on for your business.

"If you would plant for days, plant flowers

If you would plant for years, plant trees

If you would plant for eternity, plant ideas."

Key ideas to work on

List down the 5 ideas that you are going to take from this book and implement into your business.

1.____

2.____

3.____

4.____

5.____

APPENDIX

12-month learning program all in the one book

Online electronic coaching program

I know that reading a book can be a passive way to learn and to develop yourself. I have designed this program to support you in your quest for greater customer loyalty, maximising your marketplace and working smarter. This program is an online learning program designed to give you additional information and to reinforce the ideas that I have put forward in this book. There are two programs you can log on to right now without any additional cost. All you have to do is visit my website, enroll in the program with your name, e-mail address and the appropriate password and you will be receiving this online coaching before you know it. Here are the details for you to review.

Weekly loyalty ideas reinforcement program - free

This program has been designed to give you a weekly reminder of the key messages of this book, in order to refocus you on the activities that count in your business. To enrol in this program your password: Loyal Customers.

Weekly motivational message - free

These motivational messages have been designed to give your week some additional momentum. Leadership is about having momentum towards a specific goal. Each message will give you the focus you need to make things happen in your life and business. The password for this program: Passion.

Quarterly newsletter - The Passion Report - free

Each quarter we produce a widely read newsletter with articles, interviews and success stories relating to sales, service, loyalty, teamwork, and goal setting. If you would like to receive this newsletter please send me an E-mail, fax or contact our office and you will receive that with our compliments. This is available via email or throught the post.

Customer loyalty resource centre for your business

- Copy writer and direct marketing expert

  Words That Sell - Kris Fitzsimmons - Managing Director, - 0408 068 712

- Cartoons

  Scoop Media - The Cartoon Bank - (02) 9973 1603

- Audio tape/video production

  McGirvan Media - Alan McGirvan - (07) 3257 0400

- Newsletter articles

  People Pursuing A Passion - (07) 3848 56 46 or Visit Our Website at www.keithabraham.net.au

- Venue organiser

  Online Events - www.venuefinders.com.au

- Useful websites

  Electronic Greeting Cards - www.bluemountain.com

  Useless Facts - www.uselessfacts.net

  Famous Quotes - www.Sperience.com

- Great postcards and customer contact system

  Prospex Profile - (07) 5574 3000 or you can e-mail them prospexmail@prospex.com.au

- Automated online customer contact programs

  Firststep Communications - Gihan Perera - Managing Director (08) 9444 1225 or you can e-mail him at gihan@firststep.com.au for more information.

Resources available from the People Pursuing A Passion website - www.keithabraham.net.au

The following is some of the information available to assist you in developing your business to its full potential.

- Electronic online coaching program
  - Monthly loyalty message program enrolment - free of charge and the password for this program: Loyal Customers.
  - Weekly motivational message - free of charge and the password for this program: passion.
  - Monthly Earn More, Work Less program - 12 months and you can enrol via our website
  - Weekly Power, Passion, Pizzazz program - 12 months and you can enrol via our website

- Agenda for conducting a customer feedback meeting

- Customer survey prototype

- Questions for your customer's needs analysis

- Telephone script for approaching your referrals

- Recommended reading list for business leaders

- Professional business building tools catalogue

Where we can be contacted

office: 61 7 **3848 5646**

fax: *61* 7 3892 7493

email address: loyalty@keithabraham.net.au

web site: www.keithabraham.net.au

postal: PO Box 3152, Yeronga Q. 4104 Australia

Keith's Background...

In 1999 Keith was awarded the title of Certified Speaking Professional (CSP) by the National Speakers Association, which makes him one of the top 25 speakers in Australia working with some of the 'Who's Who' of business.

One of the things that makes Keith different from many keynote speakers is that he really does 'walk his talk', practicing what he preaches. Keith is a unique, entertaining and impactful speaker who uses the latest "high tech" multi media presentation methods, experiential activities, accelerated learning and practical skills to deliver powerful, thought provoking messages and empowering principles.

He is a product of his own teachings, from his humble beginnings, to a manager of 65 staff with a $15 million budget, to these days working with some of Australia's who's who in business.

Keith has a record second to none when it comes to achieving results and coaching individuals towards their true potential. He has achieved some phenomenal results in his business career.

He has created a fantastic business built on nothing but referrals. Four and a half years ago, he started with no clients working from his home in Brisbane which had a silent telephone number. Today he still works from his home and has over 141 clients which he works with on a regular basis around Australia and overseas.

Customised presentations that achieve results...

Client Loyalty - Winning Them and Keeping Them

- The 22 Ways to Get Your Clients to Pursue Your Product with a Passion
- How to turn one time buyers into Raving Fans

Procrastinator Eliminator - Goal Setting

- The 4 Ways to Have Unwavering Personal Focus and a Passion for Excellence
- 6 Steps to having Power, Passion and Pizzazz in Your Life

Strategically Selling

- The 7 Simple Steps to Turn a Prospect into a Lifetime Client
- 3 Part Formula to Double Your Income, with 80% less effort

Customer Service - Do you have it?

- How to Go from Acceptable Service to Exceptional Service
- How to get Your People to Have Passion to Service Your Customers

Team Building - Indoor/Outdoor

- A 9 Step Model on How to Have Your Team Passionate About Your Company
- 4 Ways to Get Individuals to Take Ownership and to Gain Synergy

Businesses that have benefited from Keith...

AMP
A.L.H. Group
Australian Insurance Institute
Brisbane BMW
Chrysler Jeep Australia
Conrad Treasury
Hotel & Casino
Couriers Please
Dreamworld
FAI Insurance Group
Mercantile Mutual
Lumley Insurance
I.F.M.A. Financial Services
Franchise Council of Australia
Heidelberg Australia
Heidelberg New Zealand
I.B.M Australia
L.J Hooker
Queensland Nursery
Association
Rydges Hotels & Resorts
S.P.H.C. Group
Taxi Council of Queensland
Terry White Group
Warner Brothers Movieworld
Westpac Banking & Finance